The Dynamic Individualism
of William James

The Dynamic Individualism
of William James

JAMES O. PAWELSKI

State University of New York Press

Published by
State University of New York Press, Albany

For information, contact State University of New York Press, Albany, NY
www.sunypress.edu

Production by Ryan Morris
Marketing by Michael Campochiaro

Library of Congress Cataloging-in-Publication Data

Pawelski, James O., 1967–
    The dynamic individualism of William James / James O. Pawelski.
        p. cm.
    Includes bibiographical references and index.
    ISBN: 978-0-7914-7240-8 (pbk. : alk. paper)
    ISBN: 978-0-7914-7239-2 (hardcover : alk. paper)
    1. James, William, 1842–1910. 2. Individualism. I. Title.

B945.J24P20 2007
191—dc22   2006100302

10 9 8 7 6 5 4 3 2 1

For John Lachs,
model, mentor, means of grace

Contents

Acknowledgments

Although this book was written in solitude, it would never have been completed without the help of many dynamic individuals. To thank each adequately here is impossible; it would require a separate volume at least as long as this one.

I have benefited greatly from the wisdom, knowledge, and nurture of a great many teachers, mentors, and advisors. Among them are Douglas R. Anderson, James Campbell, Vincent Michael Colapietro, Mihaly Csikszentmihalyi, Hermann Deuser, Richard M. Gale, William Joseph Gavin, Peter H. Hare, Richard E. Hart, Carl R. Hausman, Robert E. Innis, Dale Jacquette, Carl S. Keener, John J. McDermott, Gary J. Percesepe, Christopher Peterson, Paul Pyle, Martin E. P. Seligman, Richard Shusterman, John J. Stuhr, George E. Vaillant, and Carl G. Vaught.

A host of friends and colleagues have supported me in big and small ways. I am especially grateful to Stacey Ake, Dana Arakawa, Jeff Barker, Sue Borelli, John Danisi, Alberta Ferrario, Gina Frieden, Jason Grim, Maya Gupta, Donna Hancock, Julie Hess, Thea Kokubun, Colin Koopman, Jeff Leach, Ruth Margraff, Beth Ondo, Betsy Rodriguez, Melanie Schmidt, Deb Schussler, John Shook, Christina Slenk, Jan Staab, Michael Stahl, Debbie Swick, and Amy Wenzel. Holly Marshall and Sharon Rider, in particular, have taught me much about epiphanic experience.

I have been very fortunate to have the support and encouragement of my parents John and Ruth Pawelski over many years. I am very thankful for their love and for the many important things they have taught me. I am also grateful for the increasing closeness I have felt with each of my siblings: Hope, Dan, and Paul.

I would like to acknowledge the outstanding support of the folks at State University of New York Press. The professionalism and collegiality of my editor Jane Bunker, my production editor Ryan Morris, and their staff have made the process of publishing this book remarkably smooth and surprisingly easy. Excellent suggestions made by reviewers of the book have allowed me to improve it in significant ways. I am grateful to them for their time and insights, but, at the same time, I acknowledge responsibility for whatever faults and short-comings may remain in the text.

Versions of some of the material in this book have appeared (usually in much different form) in the following places:

"William James and Epiphanal Experience," in D. A. Crosby and C. D. Hardwick, eds., *Religion in a Pluralistic Age: Proceedings of the Third International Conference on Philosophical Theology*. New York: Peter Lang, 2001, 277–88.

"William James's Divided Self and the Process of Its Unification: A Reply to Richard Gale," *Transactions of the Charles S. Peirce Society*, 39:4 (2003), 645–56.

"William James, Positive Psychology, and Healthy-Mindedness," *The Journal of Speculative Philosophy (New Series)*, 17:1 (2003), 53–67.

"Is Healthy-Mindedness Healthy?" *Cross Currents*, 53:3 (2003), 404–12.

"William James and the Journey toward Unification," *Transactions of the Charles S. Peirce Society*, 40:4 (2004), 787–802.

Finally, I have benefited personally, intellectually, and profession-ally from an extraordinary mentor, colleague, and friend. John Lachs is an individual of great zest, wisdom, and personal and social intel-ligence. Over many years, he has used these strengths to nurture, encourage, and advise a vast number of students and colleagues. That I am among this number is one of the most felicitous facts of my life—and a direct cause of the existence of this book. It is in profound appreciation and gratitude that I dedicate this book to him.

Abbreviations of the
Works of William James

The Works of William James. Edited by Frederick H. Burkhardt, Fredson Bowers, and Ignas K. Skrupskelis. Cambridge: Harvard University Press, 1975–1988. The original date of publication is given in parentheses.

PP   *The Principles of Psychology*, 3 vols., 1981 (1890)
PBC   *Psychology: Briefer Course*, 1984 (1892)
WB   *The Will to Believe*, 1979 (1897)
TT   *Talks to Teachers on Psychology*, 1983 (1899)
VRE   *The Varieties of Religious Experience*, 1985 (1902)
P   *Pragmatism*, 1975 (1907)
PU   *A Pluralistic Universe*, 1977 (1909)
SPP   *Some Problems of Philosophy*, 1979 (1911)
ERM   *Essays in Religion and Morality*, 1982
EP   *Essays in Psychology*, 1983

Also abbreviated in the text:

MS   *Memories and Studies.* New York: Longmans, 1911.
LWJ   *The Letters of William James.* Edited by H. James. Vol. 1. Boston: Atlantic Monthly Press, 1920.
CWL   *The Correspondence of William James.* Edited by Ignas K. Skrupskelis and Elizabeth M. Berkely, with the assistance of Bernice Grohskopf and Wilma Bradbeer. 12 vols. Charlottesville: University Press of Virginia, 1992–2004.

Introduction

It would be difficult to dispute the claim that William James is an individualist. James himself claims to be a "rabid individualist" (CWJ, 9:625), and in a wide variety of works published over many years, he maintains that the individual is the primary starting point for understanding the world. He writes, for example, "Surely the individual, the person in the singular number, is the more fundamental phenomenon, and the social institution, of whatever grade, is but secondary and ministerial" (MS, 102). In his classic *Principles of Psychology*, James argues that the proper object of a psychologist's study is the finite, individual mind. He holds that "the mind which the psychologist studies is the mind of distinct individuals inhabiting definite portions of a real space and of a real time" (PP, 183). James also defends the status of the individual in his writings on religion. In *The Varieties of Religious Experience*, he writes: "I think . . . that however particular questions connected with our individual destinies may be answered, it is only by acknowledging them as genuine questions, and living in the sphere of thought which they open up, that we become profound" (VRE, 394).

In addition to these personal claims from James himself, commentators agree both that James is an individualist and that his individualism is central to his philosophical views. Concerning James's social philosophy, Ralph Barton Perry writes that, for James, "value derives ultimately from the interests of the individual; and the social whole is justified by the inclusion and reconciliation of its individual parts. Individualism is fundamental."[1] With respect to James's psychology, John Danisi maintains that it is James's "avowed aim and central message" to begin with finite, individual minds.[2] John E. Smith points out James's individualism and its centrality for his pragmatism: "James defended the uniqueness and irreducibility of the individual self. The hallmark of James's pragmatism is its uncompromising belief in each person's right, and even duty, to take his own experience seriously and to use it as a touchstone for thought and action."[3] John

J. McDermott describes in the strongest terms the individualism that appears throughout James's writings. He claims that "the basic cast of [James's] thought runs not only against social conglomerates but against simple aggregates as well. . . . James was an unabashed and indefatigable champion of sheer individuality."[4]

It is easy to see, both from James's own claims and from the observations of his commentators, that James is an individualist. Proceeding beyond this easy labeling, however, we find that it is quite difficult to determine just what *kind* of individualist he is. Although individualism is one of the most basic and persistent themes in James's thought, he himself never makes a formal presentation of his views on the matter. Instead, he is content to discuss his individualism piecemeal, as it comes up in various contexts. This is not surprising, since James's writing is more often motivated by a particular, inspiring interest than by the goal of a systematic presentation of an architectonic. What *is* surprising, though, is that this central aspect of James's thought has yet to be carefully and systematically explored. To this point, commentators have typically been content to accept it as an unproblematic label, hardly more than mentioning its influence on some aspect of his thought.

I believe it is important not only to know *that* James is an individualist, but also to understand what *kind* of individualist he is. Because individualism is such an important and pervasive part of James's thought, gaining clarity about the precise nature of the individualism he develops will help us understand better the areas of his thought it underlies—including his views on sociology, psychology, religion, and metaphysics.

My purpose here is to carry out a careful study of James's individualism. Because the secondary literature on this topic is sparse, this study will require an extensive search through James's own writings. Secondary literature will help shed light on certain parts of the study, but in the main it will consist of an exploration of James's individualism in the wide variety of texts in which he explicitly or implicitly takes up the topic.

The thesis I will defend throughout this study is that James's individualism is dynamic, and that it is dynamic in three specific ways. First, it is diachronically dynamic in that it changes over the course of his career. Second, it is organically dynamic in that it is rooted in his physiology. Third, it is developmentally dynamic in that it has as one of its central concerns the growth of the individual.

A look at the Jamesian corpus reveals three general contexts in which James discusses individualism. First is the social context, in which he examines the relations among individuals in a community.

James focuses on these relations mainly in lectures that were subsequently collected and published in *The Will to Believe* and *Memories and Studies*. Second is the psychological context, in which James takes up the relations among the various faculties within each individual psyche. He has much to say about these relations in the two volumes of his *Principles of Psychology*. Third is the metaphysical context, in which James analyzes the relations between the individual and the larger spiritual reality of which he considers it to be a part. This context should be understood as metaphysical in the broad sense of concerning itself with ultimate reality. Because James holds both that religious experience is our chief means of accessing ultimate reality and that individuals are constitutive of that reality, I include James's discussions of religion in this metaphysical context. Thus, I take this context to include James's religious treatment of the individual in *The Varieties of Religious Experience*, as well as his defense of radical empiricism in *A Pluralistic Universe*.

One possible way to carry out this study would be to examine the internal psychological relations of individuals first and then to move to their external social relations and their eternal metaphysical relations. Ordering the study in this way would have the advantage of beginning with the individual James defends and moving toward the social and metaphysical arenas in which he carries out his defense.

I have chosen not to proceed in this way. I believe there are greater advantages to beginning with the sociological and then moving to the psychological and metaphysical dimensions of James's individualism. One such advantage is a function of James's understanding of the relation between the psychological and the metaphysical realms. For James, access to the metaphysical is largely through the subconscious, so that there is a sense in which the eternal relations of the individual can be seen as even deeper internal relations than the psychological ones. Beginning with James's sociological discussion and moving to his psychological and then to his metaphysical discussions allows the study of James's individualism to proceed in a single direction, from what is outermost to what is innermost.

Another advantage that arises from beginning with the sociological is that the study of James's individualism then proceeds from the less complex to the more complex in his account. We will begin with the sociological, which is relatively straightforward; move to the psychological, which includes greater richness and some tension; and then turn to the metaphysical, which contains not only the greatest richness but also severe tension. This growing tension itself will need to be addressed before this study is concluded.

I propose to carry out this study in three parts. Part I consists of an exploration of James's individualism in the various texts in which he discusses its external, internal, and eternal dimensions. Part II consists of an attempt to interpret this individualism in light of the tensions discovered through this exploration and in light of the work of previous scholars in trying to understand the tensions that pervade James's writings. Part III consists of an application of my interpretation of James's individualism, an exploration of what James might call the "cash value" of the approach I argue for in Part II.

Part I consists of three chapters, in each of which we will consider one of the domains in which James discusses his individualism. Chapter 1 is an analysis of the sociological dimensions of this individualism. In this chapter, we will consider James's views on the relation of individuals to other individuals. We will begin by looking at James's theory of social evolution, where he gives a detailed explanation of the roles various individuals must play if society is to progress. We will then explore how James's individualism applies to four different communities within society: the scientific, the governmental, the religious, and the academic. Because institutions play a particularly significant role in the last three of these communities, we will examine James's views on the relation between individuals and institutions. We will find that, although James acknowledges the important roles played by some institutions in society, he tries to protect individuals from abuse by these institutions.

Chapter 2 is an analysis of the psychological dimensions of the individuals James is interested in protecting. In his description of consciousness, we will see a bit of tension begin to emerge. On the one hand, James is committed to the continuity of the "stream of consciousness"; on the other hand, he recognizes the importance of the selectivity of consciousness. On the one hand, consciousness is a continuous and ever-changing stream; on the other hand, we have the ability to select out certain parts of the stream for special attention and use. In his psychology, James tries to resolve this tension by means of the reflex action theory of the self. James takes the theory of reflex action from physiology and applies it extensively—sometimes literally and sometimes figuratively—in his psychology and elsewhere. In its physiological form, the reflex action theory distinguishes between incoming and outgoing nerve impulses in the bodies of animals. Incoming sensory impulses bring information about the world to a centralized location where they are reflected into outgoing motor impulses that determine the body's physical response to the stimuli. In lower animals, reflex action is instinctual. In humans, however, this process includes conception and volition, mental functions whose application is at the flexion point between incoming and outgoing impulses.

Applied to psychology, the reflex action model describes three basic functions of the human mind: perception, conception, and volition. Perception involves the introduction of novelty into the mind by means of incoming sensations; conception is the mental process of translating perceptual data into concepts; and volition is the means for determining the appropriate response to the novelty. It is also important to note in this context that the reflex action model, in effect, postulates electrochemical neural current as a physiological concomitant to James's psychological stream of consciousness. This physiological reflex arc allows for a dynamic account of how the psychological stream of consciousness can be both continuous and selective.

Chapter 3 is an analysis of the metaphysical dimensions of James's individualism. We will take a careful look at James's individualistic account of religious experience in *Varieties* and at his metaphysical theory of the relation between the human and the divine in *A Pluralistic Universe*. Our analysis will uncover considerable tension in James's views. Some of these tensions arise from an attempt to understand the precise nature of his metaphysical individualism. Although it may initially seem that James's individualism does not extend to his religious and metaphysical writings, we will see that, in reality, it does. But this fact leads to even greater tension when we try to understand James's metaphysical individualism in light of his other writings. We are left with what appear to be two very different kinds of individualisms. In his early work, James seems to espouse a "volitional individualism," in which teleology and choice are the key individuating factors. In his later religious and metaphysical writings, however, he seems to defend a "perceptual individualism," in which feeling is the key individuating factor.

The tensions that emerge from a close examination of James's individualism are too great to leave unresolved. In Part II we will address these tensions directly. The problem of their resolution is part of a larger difficulty all readers of James must face, and one we will take up in chapter 4. Insightful as James's works are, they contain vagueness, ambiguity, and inconsistency to a degree that presents serious challenges for the reader. Commentators have suggested a variety of ways for understanding these textual difficulties. A look at a number of these suggestions will show that they each have merit, but that none goes far enough in resolving these tensions. We will also note a common error to which James interpreters are prone.

In chapter 5, I offer a new way of reading James that will minimize some of the tensions in his individualism. I will propose an

"Integration Thesis," according to which James made significant progress toward resolving these tensions in the last ten years of his life. The key to the Integration Thesis is the recognition that the reflex arc plays an important role in James's thought throughout his career and across the various domains of his writing. Although James places varying emphasis on the different parts of the reflex arc, in his later works he moves toward a more balanced integration of them.

In Part III, the final section of this book, I apply James's thought to a realm of experience he touches on but does not investigate completely. Chapter 6 consists of an application of my interpretation of James's mature individualism to what I will call "epiphanic experience." Human experience includes both feelings of wholeness (moments of religious, philosophical, aesthetic, or romantic epiphany) and feelings of mundanity (the structure of everyday, ordinary existence). "Structured wholeness" is my theory for applying James's mature individualism to the various phases of epiphanic experience. According to structured wholeness, the stoic rejection of epiphany and the romantic rejection of mundanity are both pathological. It insists, instead, on the volitional integration of epiphany and mundanity in a process of limitless personal progress.

In light of this brief overview of each of the chapters in this book, I can now restate in greater detail my thesis that James's individualism is diachronically, organically, and developmentally dynamic. The diachronic dynamism of James's individualism can be seen in terms of three phases of its development. In his early psychological writings, he holds to a volitional individualism. This is a kind of existentialist position, where individuals are defined in terms of their own choices and actions. In his middle writings on religion, James holds to a perceptual individualism. Here individuals are defined in terms of their openness to nonrational and nonconscious realms of experience. In his later philosophical works, James moves toward an integrated individualism, where both activity and receptivity are emphasized as essential aspects of individual experience.

The organic dynamism of James's individualism can be seen in its dependence on the movement of the reflex arc. Just as the reflex arc is not fully functional unless perception, conception, and volition are all in balance, so, too, the individual is not fully functional without a proper relation among these components. This helps us see why volitional and perceptual individualisms are ultimately unsatisfactory. They each emphasize one area of the reflex arc and neglect the others. It is only integrated individualism that acknowledges the proper organic balance of the individual. This organic nature of James's individualism also points out the danger of characterizing James as "divided" or of seeing a "unity" in James's thought. James was less interested in division or in unity and more interested in how divisions could become unified. Indeed, James's integrated individualism emphasizes the continual "process of unification."

Finally, the developmental dynamism of James's individualism can be seen in its emphasis on growth. When perception, conception, and volition each play their proper roles, the result is an individual well equipped to negotiate the challenges of appropriating new experiences without losing the value of what has already been appropriated in the past. The result, in short, is an individual well equipped for growth.

These three ways in which James's individualism is dynamic correlate with three chief contributions to James scholarship I hope to make with this present volume. First is simply a sustained study and exploration of James's individualism. Second is an important new way of interpreting James. If it is true—as I believe it is—that an understanding of James's philosophy requires an understanding of his psychology, I argue that it is just as true that an understanding of James's psychology requires an understanding of his physiology. Keeping James's physiology (and especially his appropriation and elaboration of reflex action theory) at the center of his thinking gives us a hermeneutic key for understanding not just his discussions of individualism, but his entire corpus in fresh and dynamic ways. The third contribution I hope to make is to open up more of the "cash value" of James's dynamic, growth-oriented thought by extending its application to realms of experience James himself did not fully explore.

PART I

An Exploration of the Dynamic Individualism of William James

CHAPTER 1

External Dimensions of James's Individualism

Of all the contexts in which James discusses individualism, it is in his writings on interhuman relationships that he is most straightforward about it. In these writings, he defends the view that society must be understood in terms of its parts—its individuals—and attacks the view that individuals are to be explained in terms of the whole of society. It is important to keep in mind, however, that individualisms are not all the same. In order to understand the precise nature of the individualism James espouses, it is necessary to study in detail the particular way he holds individuals to be primary to their societies. That is the purpose of this chapter.

I will discuss James's views on the relations between individuals and their societies in five sections. In the first, I will begin examining James's social individualism by analyzing his view of the role of individuals in social evolution. According to James, there are two types of individuals involved in this evolution: geniuses and what I will call non-geniuses. These two types of individuals have different roles to play in the selection model of social evolution. According to this model (which can be seen as a variant of the reflex action model), novelty is presented, selected, and then assimilated. James holds that geniuses are those individuals who present novel ideas to a society. Non-geniuses are those who select from these novel ideas the one that will be assimilated into the structure of the society. Important to the discussion in this first section will be the question of the origin of geniuses, as well as that of their identification.

3

The last four sections of this chapter further develop the picture of James's social individualism by examining the relation between individuals and particular communities within society. The particular communities I examine are the scientific, the governmental, the religious, and the academic. Because institutions in the form of the government, the church, and the university play significant roles in the life of the last three of these communities and because James has much to say about them, their discussion will raise the question of James's view of the proper role of institutions in society.

THE INDIVIDUAL AND SOCIETY

James gives his clearest account of the roles of genius and non-genius in "Great Men and Their Environment," first published in 1880 and reprinted later in *The Will to Believe*. In this article, he argues against Herbert Spencer's view of the causes of social evolution. Spencer's view is that environmental conditions determine what changes a society will undergo, and that individual contributions are properly not assigned to the individuals themselves, but to the environment that formed them. James claims this view is unscientific, as well as mistaken, and argues for the rival view that societies change as a result of the "accumulated influences of individuals" (WB, 164).

James is not entirely clear in this essay to what extent he holds the influences of individuals to be the *exclusive* catalysts of social change. In stating his thesis, he claims of a community different in one generation from what it was in another, "The difference is due to the accumulated influences of individuals, of their examples, their initiatives, and their decisions" (WB, 164). This seems to imply that individuals are the *sole* cause of social change. Later, in a footnote, he admits that the individuals' environment shapes them to some degree through its educative influence (WB, 170, n. 3). Still later, he writes, "The fermentative influence of geniuses must be admitted as, at any rate, one factor in the changes that constitute social evolution" (WB, 172). Here James seems to weaken his conclusion to the view that individual influences are one cause among many that result in social change.

Whether or not James believes that individuals are the sole catalysts of social change, he is convinced that the relation between individuals and their social and physical environments is not one of mere dependence. Individuals may, indeed, be influenced by their environment, but they have something to contribute to that environment that they did not originally derive from it. In James's terms, individuals belong to a different cycle of operation from their environment. Although an omniscient knower would not have to distinguish between different cycles of operation, such distinctions are, for James, an essential part of human knowledge. Exploring further the difference between finite and infinite knowledge will help us understand better James's notion of cycles of operation, a notion that is central to his individualism.

James himself believes in free will, but he grants, for the sake of argument, that all human actions are determined. On this supposition, an omniscient and omnipresent being would rightly see remote environmental occurrences as causes of concrete occurrences in the human sphere. James takes as an example the case of a little boy who throws a rock at a sparrow and kills it. An eternal being might cite among the causes of this action the configuration of the Milky Way, the Constitution of the United States, and the early history of Europe. However, human beings cannot be infinitely concrete. We can think universally only by thinking abstractly. If we want to think concretely, we must limit ourselves to a specific part of the whole. We can either say abstractly that the boy's action is the result of the predetermined course of the universe acting in accordance with natural law, or we can remain concretely within the specific purpose of a particular inquiry. For example, if our interest in the sparrow's death is for the purpose of punishing its killer, we must consider the immediate factors that could have caused its death and leave to one side long-term astronomical and historical influences.

From a human perspective, James concludes, there are various cycles of operation, depending on our purposes. For a mycologist, the mold growing on certain biscuits in a ship's hold may be of great interest. In her study of it, she naturally disregards the nationality of the ship or the direction and purpose of its voyage. For the captain engaged in a naval battle, however, the mold growing on the biscuits is totally irrelevant. These two cycles of operation would be related only from a universal perspective (or at least from some perspective far wider than the human one). From the narrower, human perspective, they must be kept separate.

James points out that Darwin's theory of evolution involves a distinction between cycles of operation. In fact, James argues, one of Darwin's greatest insights is the distinction between the cycle of operation involved in the production of biological change and the cycle involved in its maintenance. Pre-Darwinian biologists hold that biological evolution is produced by adaptive changes of an organism to its environment. For example, the necks of giraffes are lengthened when they stretch to forage on the leaves of trees. Other adaptive changes include the strengthening of taxed muscles and the growing of calluses on persistently rubbed skin. Darwin contends that these adaptive changes pale in significance when compared to physiological changes produced through mutation and that mutational variations occur almost independently of the environment. That is, the production of change belongs to a non-environmental cycle of operation, even though the maintenance of that change has very much to do with the environment.[1]

When Darwin calls mutations "accidental variations," James argues, he does not mean to imply that they do not occur in accordance with natural law. He means, rather, that the changes are remote from environmental factors. Perhaps if we knew the total system of the universe, we would be able to trace the connection between the birth of a giraffe with a peculiarly long neck and the environment into which it was born. From a human perspective, however, we separate these situations into two cycles of operation. The variation occurs irrespective of the social, political, or physical environment. From the standpoint of the environmental cycle, we must accept the variation as a given and then proceed to the question of whether, through natural and sexual selection, the environment will maintain or destroy the variation.

In a similar way, James holds that the causes of production of great men and women lie in a cycle of operation different from that in which a sociologist works. A sociologist must accept geniuses as given, just as Darwin accepts spontaneous variations as given. The sociologist's proper inquiry is not into the origins of genius, but into the interplay between geniuses and their environment. Although the social environment does affect a genius through socialization and education, its main relation to genius is one of selection.

A society, James points out, is capable of development in a number of ways. The great individuals in a society use their creativity and influence to suggest certain specific alternatives, and the society selects which one to follow. Of course, a society is more positively disposed toward certain types of suggestions than it is toward others. But this is largely due to its having followed geniuses in previous generations. These past selections have closed off certain possibilities and opened up new ones. Thus, social change involves an interplay between two different cycles of operation: the genius—a product of physiological and infrasocial forces—who creates certain specific alternatives; and the social environment, which accepts or rejects the suggestions of a particular genius. James writes of these two cycles of operation and their interplay, "Both factors are essential to change. The community stagnates without the impulse of the individual. The impulse dies away without the sympathy of the community" (WB, 174). Although James's claim that geniuses are the catalysts of social change shows him to be an individualist, it is clear that he is not defending "sheer" individualism, since he emphasizes the dependence of the creative ideas of geniuses on communal selection for survival.

After establishing the importance of the individual cycle of operation, James is in a position to show why he holds the arguments of thinkers such as Herbert Spencer and Grant Allen to be unscientific. These men claim that the environment is solely responsible for social evolution. If by "environment" they mean "the outward cycle of visible nature and man," James contends, their claim is simply incorrect. He argues, first, that it fails to take into consideration the physiological cycle of operation. Second, James points out that their claim fails to distinguish between necessary and sufficient conditions of change. Certain geographical features of an environment may be necessary for a people to develop in a certain way. But it is possible to respond in a variety of ways to the same geographical parameters. An arctic climate, for example, necessitates industry. But it is not sufficient in itself to determine whether that industry will be peaceful, as in the case of the Eskimos, or warlike, as in the case of the Norsemen. Third, James holds that it does not fit the facts of actual communities. New Guinea, James contends, is very similar to Borneo in size, geological features, climate, and flora, but it is very different from Australia in these ways. According to Spencer and Allen, we would expect the fauna of New Guinea to resemble that of Borneo and to differ from that of Australia. Empirical investigation shows that, in fact, the opposite is the case and casts doubt on their theory. James raises a similar problem with respect to the human populations of Corsica and Sardinia. Because the physical conditions of these two islands are very favorable, it is to be expected that their human populations would have distinguished themselves over against their neighbors. The physical conditions of Sardinia, in particular, are superior to those of Sicily. Once again, the fact that Sicily has played a significant role in world events, while Corsica and Sardinia have rarely appeared in the pages of world history, argues against the claim that the environment is the sole determiner of social development. James concludes that the vast differences in the histories of these islands are due to the individual cycle of operation. That is, great men in Sicily pointed out the way toward the greatness of the society; whereas, Corsica and Sardinia lacked such men of genius to guide them.[2]

If, on the other hand, by "environment" Spencer and Allen mean "the whole of nature," James argues that their claim then resembles

Eastern mysticism far more than it does science. Their ultimate explanation for any event must be a vague appeal to the ultimate conditions of the universe. According to James, this appeal is a fatalistic pantheism that is more a metaphysical presupposition or an emotional stance toward the universe than it is a scientific explanation.

At this point, James's basic understanding of the relation between geniuses and their environment should be clear. Although it is true that an individual is influenced by the environment through processes such as socialization and education, James maintains that an individual's insights are not determined by that environment. Specific insights are produced by great men and women and may be preserved by the society. I have already pointed out that James is not clear to what extent he believes these insights are the *only* catalysts of social change. It seems reasonable, however, to interpret this ambiguity in James's account in accordance with Darwin's position. Just as Darwin admitted that there are adaptive changes but argued that the changes due to spontaneous variation are much more important for evolution, so I think James would admit that there are factors in social evolution other than individual influences but argue that it is these that are the most important.

This basic understanding of James's views leads to two very important questions. First, who are the "great men and women" in a society? We know that these geniuses are highly creative persons with original suggestions for the way a society ought to develop. But how can these geniuses be identified in a particular society? James does not speak directly to this question, so it is necessary to formulate a Jamesian answer based on his indirect treatment of the issue. Of course, there is no difficulty in identifying the geniuses who have been selected by a society. Their names appear in the society's history books, or, if they are still alive, in its newspapers. These geniuses have talents in different areas. Some are political geniuses; some are artistic geniuses; some are military geniuses. In rare cases, an individual may be a genius in more than one area. Usually, however, political geniuses are artistic non-geniuses, and artistic geniuses are military non-geniuses.

Easy as it is to recognize selected geniuses, non-selected geniuses can be very difficult to identify. This identification, however, is as important as it is difficult, since non-selected geniuses are potential selected geniuses. Without this identification, it is unclear how a society should allocate its scarce resources of support. Competitions, tournaments, and other contests are methods societies often use to identify these important individuals.

The difficulty of identification is made greater by the fact that the proper categorization of individuals is dependent, in part, on social context. For example, there are many individuals who are not international geniuses but who are geniuses in their particular country or city or in a particular political or religious organization. In fact, if the society is defined in narrow enough terms, there is a sense in which all individuals can be considered geniuses. Thus, the important task of identifying potential selected geniuses often involves less the mere identification of genius than the identification of individuals who have genius to the degree required by the social context in question.

This leads to an important point about the categories James creates and the distinctions he draws in his work. They often resemble his definition of genius in that they collapse under the right kind of pressure. We have just seen how, careful as James is to set up genius as a special category of individuals in a society, there is a sense in which all individuals can be considered geniuses. In chapter 2 we will see, similarly, that in his psychological writings James states in the strongest terms the psychological isolation of each individual and then softens that isolation by suggesting ways in which the borders of individuality can be crossed. In his writings on religion, to consider an example we will discuss in great detail in chapter 3, James takes great pains to distinguish between healthy-minded and morbid-minded religion and between once-born and twice-born types of individuals. Later, he blurs the first distinction by claiming that it is an abstraction and that most people are a mixture of healthy-mindedness and morbid-mindedness. He then blurs the second distinction by stating that the classification of an individual as of the once-born or of the twice-born type is often quite arbitrary.

These examples point to James's special use of categories. On the one hand, he sees certain general distinctions in a topic of inquiry and finds it helpful to create categories to describe these distinctions. Wanting to remain true to the facts, however, James never lets himself be beguiled by these categories. He sees that there are cases that fit the categories only imperfectly. A more systematic and rationalistic thinker might ignore such cases in order to preserve the neatness of the categories. In James's hands, to the contrary, it is the neatness of the category that is sacrificed to do justice to the individual cases. By keeping in mind James's approach toward categorical thinking and by understanding the reasoning behind it, we can understand better what can and what cannot be reasonably expected from a Jamesian category.

The second question that arises from James's discussion of the genius cycle of operation concerns the actual value of the contributions of geniuses. If it is true that the universe is determined, an omniscient and omnipresent being would be able to see that the contributions of geniuses are completely determined and are not novel, unique, or irreducible. James's distinction between cycles of operation would concern merely finite perspectives of the universe. That is, the contributions of geniuses would seem important to us only because of our limited perspective. Whether or not Spencer's position is merely a metaphysical presupposition or an emotional stance toward the universe, he would be right in claiming that the contributions of geniuses are nothing other than functions of their environment.

There are seeds in this early article of views James develops later. Using terms from these more developed views, we can see that James's point here is that, even if we grant that the universe is a deterministic, block universe, pluralism and individualism still have their place. James points out that Darwin's distinction between spontaneous variation and environmental selection is a pluralistic move, and he recommends to Spencer and other sociologists that they make a similar pluralistic distinction between the origin and the selection of genius. Even if the universe is completely determined, James argues, the human perspective is too limited to understand that determinism concretely. Human endeavors such as natural science and sociology must recognize human limitations. These endeavors make progress precisely by remaining within the boundaries fixed by such limitations. Thus, James's argument is that, even on the assumption that the universe is determined—an assumption James grants Spencer only for the sake of argument—pluralism must not be abandoned.

In a deterministic universe, the limitation of human knowledge results in an uneasy tension between an abstract notion of the way the universe "really is" and the concrete knowledge we humans can have of it. Spencer and others try to resolve this tension by giving up the human perspective. Although it appears that individuals change society, they argue, individuals are merely puppets in the hands of the environment. James's response to this tension is just the opposite. His commitment to the reality and meaningfulness of human experience is of the highest order. Instead of giving up the human perspective, he rejects the abstract picture determinism paints of the way the universe "really is" and develops a pluralistic view of the universe that does not seek to displace the concrete. James rejects both determinism and the existence of an omniscient and omnipresent knower of the universe. For him, cycles of operation form real barriers in the universe and are not mere functions of the limited nature of human knowledge. Thus, geniuses are not determined, and their contributions are cases of true novelty.

In "Great Men and Their Environment" James is on the defensive, criticizing monism. Even if the universe is determined, he contends, human endeavors as revered as natural science and as new as sociology must proceed pluralistically. Even if this is not the way the universe really is, it is the way natural science and sociology really are. In subsequent works, James takes the offensive, developing his pluralistic view of the universe. As we proceed, we will see that James holds that the universe "really is," like our knowledge of it, pluralistic. On this view, the finite perspectives of natural science and sociology are functions, not of a faulty human perspective, but of the pluralism inherent in the universe. This is a point to which I will return in chapter 3 and that forms a crucial part of James's mature individualism, which I will formulate in detail in Part II. For the present, I will continue tracing out the social aspects of James's pluralism, since these are also important for understanding the precise nature of his individualism.

Having examined James's views on the evolution of society in general, we are in a position to see how he applies these views to his understanding of the proper functioning of the smaller scientific, governmental, religious, and academic communities within society at large. Taking up the scientific community first, we will see that scientific progress, which follows a pattern similar to that of social evolution in general, poses a particular threat to individual freedom of belief.

THE INDIVIDUAL AND THE SCIENTIFIC COMMUNITY

It is easy to see how James's pattern of social progress applies to the scientific community. Great scientists develop theories, which, although they take advantage of the research of other scientists, are nevertheless products of their individual genius. They then present these theories to the larger community of scientists, which ultimately decides whether the new theories will be accepted or rejected. James's writings on the scientific community, however, do not focus on the details of how this process works or on citing historical examples to prove that this pattern is followed. Instead, James concentrates his energies on curbing what he sees as abuses perpetrated by all too many members of this community.

Because of its great and lasting contributions to human knowledge, science enjoys a great deal of authority in our society. It is a standing temptation for scientists to attempt to apply this authority beyond scientific matters to other areas of human experience. James has little patience for scientists who yield to this temptation. He devotes much energy to trying to keep his fellow scientists from dictating to individuals what they should believe in contexts in which, James holds, science has no legitimate authority.

James does not, of course, dispute the great range of legitimate authority science does have. As a scientist himself, he has a great appreciation for the painstaking work of thousands of persons over the hundreds of years that modern science has been in existence. The scientific method they used has proved to be a most effective way to investigate our physical environment, and the moral integrity that, for the most part, characterized the founders of science adds to its prestige. For these reasons, its conclusions carry great weight over against any subjective pretensions of individuals (WB, 17, 49).

James argues, however, that some scientists—W. K. Clifford and T. H. Huxley among them—allow themselves to be carried away by the phenomenal success science has enjoyed and attempt to put in place what he calls the "scientific veto." These scientists believe that science is the only source of valid belief and that it has a right to forbid individuals to adopt beliefs except on the basis of coercive scientific evidence. Clifford contends, for example, "It is wrong always, everywhere, and for anyone, to believe anything upon insufficient evidence" (quoted in WB, 18). Where such evidence is lacking, Clifford maintains, we must remain in doubt.

In his various writings, James marshals four arguments against the scientific veto. First, the veto is self-contradictory; second, neither science nor its practitioners have the authority to implement it; third, science itself does not follow the veto; and fourth, some nonscientific beliefs are unavoidable. It is important to examine these arguments in more detail, not only for a better understanding of James's views on the proper relation between the individual and the scientific community, but also because of their connection with James's psychological and metaphysical writings to which we will turn in subsequent chapters.

In support of his first argument that the scientific veto is self-contradictory, James discusses the relation of science to that which still lies beyond its borders. Some of James's scientific colleagues go so far as to say that science has made all of the foundational discoveries, which, lacking only certain details, will soon lead to the final truth about the universe. But James points out that such a view of science fails to take into account the facts that modern science is only a few centuries old and that it continues to make fundamental discoveries. A realistic view of science shows that its task is far from completion. Science is still surrounded by a vast sea of ignorance it has yet to explore. Thus, whatever this sea contains, and whether or not science will eventually be able to explore it in its entirety, we can be certain that the world of our present knowledge is only a part of some larger world, a world that, at present, is a mystery to us.

Scientists such as Clifford and Huxley, whom James calls agnostic positivists, maintain that we must respond with neutrality to this larger world. Since it is a mystery to us, we must remain skeptical about its contents until we acquire adequate scientific knowledge about it. But this scientific veto, James argues, is self-contradictory. It lacks scientific justification itself. The scientific veto is merely a statement of personal preference on the part of some scientists. The first step in applying the veto would be the declaration that the veto itself is unscientific and for this reason illegitimate.[3]

James's second argument is that, even if the veto were not self-contradictory, science would not have the authority to impose a limitation of this sort on individual belief. Science can make legitimate claims concerning matters that have been adequately studied by scientists, but it cannot make legitimate pronouncements about things that have not yet been adequately studied.

Third, in a move that anticipates the work of Thomas Kuhn, James argues that scientific progress depends, in part, on nonscientific motivations, desires, and beliefs. Science would not have enjoyed its great success had it not been for investigators who stubbornly demanded that the apparent chaos of the world reveal itself in an orderly, rational way. Moreover, the best investigators are not disinterested observers; rather, they have a great interest that the universe reveal itself in a particular way. That is, the best investigators are those who, while they are careful to avoid deception, want to see their hypotheses confirmed. James concludes that science is actually driven by psychological desires and beliefs that the scientific veto would not allow (WB, 21–2, 55–6).

The final reason why James considers it illegitimate for scientists to attempt to impose the scientific veto is that the veto is impossible to follow in practical matters. Concerning purely theoretical matters, we may believe, disbelieve, or doubt a certain proposition. Consider, for example, the fifth theorem of the first book of Euclid: "In isosceles triangles the angles at the base are equal to one another, and, if the equal straight lines be produced further, the angles under the base will be equal to one another."[4] Most persons who are familiar with Euclidean geometry believe in the truth of this *pons asinorum*. Of course, it is possible to disbelieve this theorem despite the wrath and pejorative epithets this would draw from those who believe it. A middle way is also open. Those who know nothing about Euclidean geometry may doubt the theorem. They may lack both a belief and a disbelief in it. Because geometrical theorems are theoretical matters, doubt is quite possible in this case. The practical life of a doubter of this theorem is unlikely to differ in any substantial way from that of a believer in it.

In practical matters, however, the case is quite different. In these situations, we must act in accordance with either belief or disbelief. We do not have the luxury of doubting. Consider, for example, the statement, "I should buy fire insurance for my house." The practical result of a theoretical *belief* in the truth of this statement is that I will buy insurance. The practical result of a theoretical *disbelief* of the statement is that I will not buy insurance. But what is the practical result of a theoretical *doubt* that the statement is true? If I doubt that buying fire insurance is a good idea, then I probably will not buy it. But this result, in the practical world, is indistinguishable from the result of outright disbelief.[5]

At this point, James's account does not seem to correspond with experience. Bertrand Russell disagrees with James's claim that there is no practical difference between doubt and disbelief. Russell points out that we "habitually act upon hypothesis, but not precisely as we act upon what we consider certainties; for when we act upon hypothesis we keep our eyes open for fresh evidence."[6] That is, the practical result of doubting a hypothesis is often different from the practical result of believing or disbelieving it. In the example we considered in the last paragraph, my doubt about the wisdom of purchasing fire insurance may lead me to consult my neighbors to see whether they have bought insurance, to confer with friends in the insurance business, or to read a book on the subject before making my decision. If my doubt and indecision remain, I may express them practically by buying a smaller amount of insurance.

Although James does not take up these objections, someone might answer for him by pointing out that, as long as I am consulting neighbors and friends and reading books, I do not have fire insurance. This practical case is a strong disjunction. Either I buy the insurance or I do not. If my house burns down and I have paid the premium, the insurance company reimburses me. If I have not paid the premium, I receive no money. There is no third way. Investigation into the wisdom of buying insurance is not so much the result of doubt whether I should buy it as it is the result of belief that I ought to investigate to find out whether or not I should. If I buy a smaller amount of insurance, my action is prompted, not by doubt, but by a belief that I should buy just that smaller amount.

Although this defense could be made for James, it is unsatisfying in that it shores up his position in a merely verbal way that leaves the real issue untouched. It tries to solve the problem by redefining what we normally consider to be doubt as belief in something else, and this redefinition leads us away from our commonsense understanding of the terms involved. For these reasons, a better response to Russell's criticism would be to admit that James overstates his case. James is quite right in showing that theoretical doubt *can* result in practical disbelief, but he goes too far by claiming that theoretical doubt *always* results in practical disbelief. There are often clear practical differences between doubt and disbelief in a given hypothesis.

Even this weaker form of James's argument, however, is strong enough to show that there are real problems with the scientific veto. Within the realm of hypotheses whose truth science is not yet in a position to decide, the rule that belief can be legitimately established only scientifically leads often (if not always) to the same practical results as the rule that we must disbelieve all such hypotheses. From a practical point of view, this seems to be a rather arbitrary way of making decisions.

In certain cases, James argues, individuals have the right to make decisions at their own risk when scientific evidence is as yet insufficient. These cases are what James calls genuine options. An option is a decision between two hypotheses, and a genuine option is an option that is living, forced, and momentous. Living options are ones in which both hypotheses seem plausible. Forced options are ones in which the alternatives are logical disjunctions, so that it is impossible to avoid making a decision. Momentous options afford unique and important opportunities.[7]

James cites moral, social, and religious questions as examples of genuine options that cannot be decided by science. Moral issues cannot be so decided, James argues, because they involve what *ought* to be the case, while science is concerned only with what *is* the case.

Social structures, James points out, require a certain faith in them on the part of their members. James observes that friendships are unlikely to develop unless both parties have faith in the other's good will. This is a case not only where the question cannot be decided scientifically, but also where the truth of the fact itself depends on a faith in the fact. If I believe that someone likes me, for example, I will tend to act toward that person in such a way as to make that belief true. James also notes that the facts our faith can help to create are not limited to the social realm. They include other cases in which the outcome of a decision is based on our personal action. James cites an example of one of these extra-social cases. Imagine that I am climbing in the Alps and that, at some point in my climb, I get myself into a dangerous situation from which I can save myself only by a difficult leap. The more I doubt the success of my jump, the more likely I will fail. My doubt will likely make me hesitate so long that when I do attempt the leap, my energy will be spent, and I will be so full of fear and doubt that I will not make it. Faith in the success of my leap, on the other hand, will likely help to make it a reality (WB, 53–4, 80).

Religious matters, too, according to James, must be decided by our passional natures. If a religious option is a living one for us, then it is a genuine option, because it is bound to be momentous and forced. Furthermore, the religious hypothesis often considers the eternal element of the universe to be personal. Thus, the religious issue becomes a social one, as well, and faith in the existence of a relationship with the personal in the universe may help to create that relationship.

Because science cannot decide genuine options of a moral, social, or religious kind, James argues, these options will be decided some other way. They cannot, by definition, go undecided. Both on a practical and on a theoretical level, any attempt to avoid deciding them ends in failure. On the practical level, the attempt to avoid deciding a genuine option has the same result as deciding one way or the other. On the theoretical level, as our study of James's psychology in the next chapter will show, the attempt to avoid believing either of the two hypotheses in a genuine option requires a volitional act of disbelief in both. In genuine options that cannot in principle be decided by the intellect, James contends that: "[Our] passional nature not only lawfully may, but must, decide . . . for to say, under such circumstances, 'Do not decide, but leave the question open,' is itself a passional decision,—just like deciding yes or no,—and is attended with the same risk of losing the truth" (WB, 20, italics deleted).

Before I move on to a discussion of James's views on religious and academic communities, I want to make some observations about his defense of the right of individuals to believe. It is important to note, first, the restrictions James puts on this right. In "The Will to Believe" James defends the individual's right to base beliefs on passional decisions only in the case of genuine options that cannot by their nature be decided on intellectual grounds. James's defense of the individual's right to believe, like his defense of the individual, is qualified.

Although James's defense is of a restricted right to believe, it is also important to note that he extends this restricted right to all individuals. Geniuses and non-geniuses alike have the same right in this regard. Although he describes differing social roles for these two classes of individuals, geniuses do not form a privileged class of persons with more individual rights than others. James's view of the individual's right to believe, like his individualism in general, is impartial.

James's defense of individual freedom of belief in the face of oppressive and illegitimate scientific encroachments is not merely of theoretical significance for him. Instead, his defense of the right to believe is motivated by his own bout with long-armed scientific doctrines that refuse to leave room for his spiritual needs and that even threaten his sanity. There are two scientific doctrines in particular whose unlimited extension threaten James's spiritual well-being.

The first of these scientific doctrines is determinism. James's fight against determinism is one of the most familiar parts of his biography. After completing his medical degree in the summer of 1869, James began to sink into a deep depression. Whatever the complex combination of its causes,[8] we can tell by its cure that it was caused, in large part, by a deterministic threat to his moral freedom. James describes the turning point of his depression in the following way:

> I think that yesterday was a crisis in my life. I finished the first part of Renouvier's second *Essais* and see no reason why his definition of free will—'the sustaining of a thought *because I choose to* when I might have other thoughts'—need be the definition of an illusion. At any rate, I will assume for the present—until next year—that it is no illusion. My first act of free will shall be to believe in free will. (LWJ, 147)

Thus, although determinism is a fruitful doctrine in many scientific pursuits, it is essential for James to keep it out of his moral life. Only with freedom of choice does he believe that life can be meaningful. Because the quest for meaning is so important to him, he fights vigorously to defend his right—and that of others—to believe in freedom.

The second scientific doctrine James fights against is materialism. Like determinism, materialism is a fruitful view to adopt in certain sciences, but it is poison to many temperaments if allowed into the spiritual realm. Materialism is especially dangerous, not only because it, too, threatens meaning, but also because it eliminates the possibility of being on intimate religious terms with the universe.

While freedom is the basis of the moralism that is so attractive to James when he is strong, nonmaterialism is the basis of the religion he needs when he is weak. When strong, James craves meaning; when weak, intimacy (see ERM, 61–3). Because both of these needs are threatened if determinism and materialism are not kept within their scientific limitations, we can see why James is so ardent in his fight against those who claim that either or both of these doctrines must be applied to all areas of life.

James's fight against the unlimited application of determinism and materialism—or, put positively, his defense of meaning and intimacy—leads to another problem to which we will return in chapter 3. The problem is that, early in life, James believes that meaning and intimacy, and the respective moralistic and religious views of the world that are based on them, are at odds. At one point, he writes, "The accord of moralism and religion is superficial, their discord radical. Only the deepest thinkers on both sides see that one must go" (ERM, 63). It is only toward the end of his life that James sees a way past the radical discord between moralism and religion and is able to integrate his needs for both meaning and intimacy. Before this integration, however, this discord results in severe tension both in James's life and in his writings.

With this examination of the personal and practical motivations for James's attacks on scientism, I will leave his discussion of the appropriate relation between individuals and the scientific community and turn to his discussion of three other communities within society: governmental, the religious, and the academic. The discussion of these three communities will bring up the question of the appropriate role of institutions in social evolution. Institutions often furnish the stage on which the roles of geniuses and non-geniuses are played. James has very specific ideas about how institutions should facilitate the drama of social change that takes place largely on their stage, and he has no tolerance for institutions that forget that this social drama is more important than their own prestige. Turning now to a discussion of James's writings on the government, the church, and the university will help shed light on what James takes to be the proper relation between individuals and institutions. This, in turn, will help us understand more deeply his views on the nature of individuals and their role in society.

THE INDIVIDUAL AND THE GOVERNMENT

Although James wrote relatively little about the government in his academic works, he did express important views on the relation between the individual and the government in various letters. Some of these were private letters to friends; others were public letters to the editor printed in various newspapers. For our present purposes, I would like to focus on two particular issues on which he expressed his opinions in this way.

The first is the issue of medical licensing. In 1894 and 1898, there were bills before the Massachusetts legislature requiring persons engaged in medical practice to be licensed. James realized that this would render illegal the work of many alternative healers who would not consent to take the examinations required for the licenses. He saw this move as misguided for several reasons, one of which was that the state of medical knowledge was far too limited for anyone to know with certainty which types of practice were truly effective. By dismissing out of hand the novel work of a host of practitioners, legislators might be cutting off a vital source of new suggestions necessary for the evolution of medical practice. On James's evolutionary model, it was better to have a rich variety of options on which experiments could be made to determine which were most effective. Geniuses in the medical world needed to be free to develop and suggest their novel ideas just as much as geniuses in any other endeavor. James felt so strongly about this that he mailed off letters to the editor in 1894 and actually went before a committee of the legislature in 1898 to make his case.

The second issue is the American imperialism that arose in the course of the Spanish-American War. Begun with the intention of liberating Cuba from Spanish imperial control, the war ended with the United States exerting imperial control in the Philippines. James was deeply disturbed by this turn of events. The United States liberated the Philippines from Spanish control, only to become the new imperial masters of the islands. American forces quelled Filipino attempts at self-government, arguing that the Filipinos simply wouldn't be able to govern themselves effectively. James saw this argument as nothing more than a thinly veiled imperialism, all the more pernicious because of its misleading moralistic whitewash. He tried to fight this imperialism by making his views heard publicly, both by publishing letters to the editor on this topic and by joining the Anti-Imperialist League.

James's defense of individual Filipinos and of their right to govern themselves brings out another important aspect of James's social individualism. James's arguments here arise less out of a concern for staying out of the way of social evolution and more out of a deep respect for concrete individual experience. James understands how difficult it can be for human beings to respect the inner experience of others, particularly of others who are significantly different from them. James develops this point in "On a Certain Blindness in Human Beings," emphasizing that it is the joy we feel in our inner experience that makes life precious. But this joy is not always correlated with external success. In fact, it often seems to make itself felt under conditions that to an outside observer would seem full of boredom or suffering. James concludes that we must not presume to judge the inner worlds of others based on our own abstract and external observations. Instead, we must respect those inner worlds (as long as they do not arise by harming others), however meaningless they may appear to us to be. James's anti-imperial position on American policy in the Philippines is a particular application of this commitment to respect the concrete experience of others.

James's responses to the medical licensing issue and to the Spanish-American War illustrate his view that individuals are important both in their own right and for the purposes of social evolution. For James, governments are institutions that should value and protect the rights and interests of all individuals, including those not under their jurisdiction. Furthermore, governments should give individual geniuses the freedom necessary to develop their ideas, protecting them against overzealous professionalisms that would seek to rule their contributions out of bounds. Indeed, James writes, "The best commonwealth will always be the one that most cherishes the man who represents the residual interests, the one that leaves the largest scope to their peculiarities" (MS, 103).

THE INDIVIDUAL AND THE CHURCH

In *The Varieties of Religious Experience*, James discusses the roles of individuals and institutions in religion. He writes little about institutional religion, and the little he does write is not positive. Early in the book, he distinguishes between what he calls institutional religion and personal religion (VRE, 32ff). He holds that the former, which he defines as an external attempt to win the favor of the gods, is a secondary and derivative form of religion; he holds the latter, by which he understands an internal and individual relationship between a person and the divinity, to be the primary form of religion. James announces that his discussion in *Varieties* will ignore institutional religion, with its ecclesiastical organization and systematic theology, and will concentrate, instead, on personal religion.

In arguing that personal religion is more fundamental than institutional religion, James points out that religious sects are founded by individuals who have had great personal religious experience. The relation between churches and religious geniuses does not depart from the pattern of variation and selection, of innovation and imitation. Religion begins in the private lives of geniuses such as the Buddha, Jesus, Mohammed, Luther, Wesley, and Fox, who have striking religious experiences. As they relate these experiences to those around them, their personal type of religion is either confirmed or rejected. When it is confirmed, a church or sect is often founded. This organization grows large or stays small, depending on how well it meets the needs of the larger social environment. But once the religion passes to this institutional phase, it loses James's interest and, apparently, his respect. He seems to consider churches to be largely inessential for religion. In fact, he holds that religious institutions that emphasize external and public worship may distract an individual from the primary, private experience, thus actually stunting the growth of religion.

Although James rejects the communities that tend to gather around great religious leaders, he does not leave religion merely in the hearts of individuals. There is an important public side of religion, although it is not in the church that this public side is addressed. James calls, not on the church, but on philosophy to distill from the various religious manifestations what he calls the "science of religions." To do this, philosophy must give up a rationalistic and deductive method for an empirical and inductive one. It must not dabble in dogmatic metaphysics, but must take as its starting point the actual experiences of religious persons. By comparing these experiences and eliminating from them the local prejudices and historical sedimentation, philosophy can distill the essential characteristics of religion. These characteristics can be turned into hypotheses for testing to try to arrive at a system of beliefs that even nonreligious persons might accept as authoritative.

James emphasizes that this science of religions is not itself to be understood as a religion. It is a theoretical foundation for the interpretation of religion. As theoretical, it is a public attempt to understand the personal. As public, it must allow for the construction of various "over-beliefs." That is, each individual must have the freedom to build his or her own idiosyncratic religious structure on the universal foundation. Individuals as diverse as Emerson, Whitman, Wesley, and Moody must all be allowed to build on this foundation. Only in this way is it possible to maintain the fullness and variety of the human experience of the divine.

James goes on to suggest what the theoretical foundation of religion might look like. From his study of firsthand accounts of religious experience, he concludes that religion is basically about an uneasiness and its solution. The solution involves an identification with a higher part of the self and a distancing from a lower part. To explain how this occurs, James offers a hypothesis to be tested by the science of religions. James's hypothesis is that the subconscious self mediates between the shallower and the deeper parts of the self.

Whether the subconscious *is* the deeper part of the self, or whether the deeper part of the self merely communicates *through* it to the shallower part of the self is beyond the scope of the science of religions to decide. On this question, individuals have a right to their own opinions in correspondence with their particular experience and over-beliefs.

Although this is as far as the science of religions can go, James—speaking as an individual with his own over-beliefs—has much more to say on the question. In the third chapter, I will come back to this point and take up James's over-beliefs in detail. For the present, it is sufficient to note his estimation of religious institutions. He seems to have little interest in or respect for the church and for institutional religion in general. Although he suggests an institutional, or at least a rational, function for the science of religions, it is important to understand that this function lies outside of religion proper. Interestingly, in his treatment of academic institutions, James is still quite critical but not as dismissive.

THE INDIVIDUAL AND THE UNIVERSITY

If the role of a genius is to develop a creative possibility and the role of society is to choose between this possibility and those created by other geniuses, what can social institutions contribute to this process? In the case of education, James argues that the university has a dual role to play. In several lectures delivered toward the end of his life and reprinted posthumously in *Memories and Studies*, James contends that the university should be both an aid to geniuses and a training ground to enable non-geniuses to discriminate wisely among geniuses. James further cautions that the university should never pretend to be more important than the individuals associated with it. A careful reading of these lectures reveals not only the details of what place James thinks the university should occupy in a society, but also what seem to be James's mature views on the proper relation between individuals and institutions in general.

In the spring semester of 1906, James was a visiting professor at Stanford University. On Founder's Day of that year, he delivered an address entitled "Stanford's Ideal Destiny." In this speech, James formulates some of the conditions for an ideal university and encourages Stanford to strive to meet those conditions. He argues that the quality of a university depends less on its facilities, boards, regulations, teaching methods, or funding than on the individuals who are there. He quotes favorably a New England quip that "a log by the roadside with a student sitting on one end of it, and Mark Hopkins sitting on the other end" is a university (MS, 361).[9] In fact, James claims, the organization of the university is largely superfluous, given the presence of a few such geniuses. The cultural and even economic value of a genius cannot be overestimated. It should, therefore, be the task of the university to invite geniuses to its faculty and to give them all the support they need to expedite their work.

A few years before his address at Stanford, James had given a speech at a Harvard commencement dinner after receiving an honorary degree. In this speech, he contrasts the "club feeling" at Harvard with what he calls the "true Harvard." The true value of a university cannot be judged by its club qualities, he contends, since students' loyalties in this respect are formed according to the school they happen to attend. Nor can a university be judged by the activities of its graduates, since its alumni can be found on every side of public debates. Rather, James argues, the most admirable university is the one that best nourishes the geniuses among its students. He writes that the university "most worthy of rational admiration is that one in which your lonely thinker can feel himself least lonely, most positively furthered, and most richly fed" (MS, 354).

James believes that the value of a university must be assessed, in part, by how many geniuses it has among its faculty and students and by how successful it is in creating a supportive environment for them. But he also believes that a university's responsibility extends beyond its duty to its geniuses. A university must also take care to educate well those of its students who are not geniuses.

In a lecture delivered to a meeting of the Association of American Alumnae at Radcliffe College in 1907, James considers the purpose of a college education for non-geniuses. According to James, the purpose of such an education is that it should "help you to know a good man when you see him" (MS, 309, italics deleted).[10] James compares a college education to vocational training. At a business, technical, or professional school, students learn concrete disciplines. More than that, however, they learn to judge the quality of work in their field. They learn what separates the work of an expert from that of a novice. The essence of a college education, James argues, should be the study of biographical history, of the successes and mistakes of great thinkers in the quest for human perfection. This study allows students to discover the standards of human excellence and to differentiate between good and mediocre thinkers.

Human progress, James continues, occurs through the initiative of geniuses and their imitation by the community. Economic, political, and intellectual circumstances serve only as the background to the human drama between a people and its leaders. In a democracy, James points out, the role of the people is all the more significant. Through their political and economic choices, the people select certain leaders and reject others. To do this effectively, the people must be skilled in knowing the difference between a good leader and a bad one. What better way, James asks, to develop this knowledge than through the study of biographical history conducted at college? For James, those with a college education in a democracy must play the role that the aristocracy plays in a monarchy. Just as the aristocracy is to preserve a taste for the more refined and noble of human achievements, so, too, college graduates must lead the people away from mediocrity and toward higher, more lasting ways of development.

In light of these arguments, it is clear that James considers the university to have a most important role to play in human progress. Ideally, it is a place where professorial geniuses can work to develop their theories untrammeled by financial cares and limitations of resources, where gifted students can educate themselves in an environment that supports them but leaves them free to do their work, and where the rest of the students are taught how to choose the best geniuses to follow. Unfortunately, universities sometimes fall far short of this ideal, especially when their leaders consider their primary purpose to be an institutional one. When the growth and prestige of the university become its ultimate goal, then it is less likely to be successful in its important function of aiding human progress. The university's proper function is vitiated when the institutional policy of the university becomes more important than the individuals who fill its posts.

As an example of a misguided institutional policy, James cites the abuse of the Ph.D., a recent arrival on the American academic scene. During his career at Harvard, James saw the tendency of the Ph.D. to be used, not as a spur to greater scholarship, but as an institutional stamp of approval. In "The Ph.D. Octopus," he speaks out against what he considers to be the abuse of higher degrees. He begins with an account of a brilliant man who had studied philosophy at the Harvard Graduate School and who acquired a position teaching literature in a small college. When it was discovered, however, that he had not completed his Ph.D., the president of the college informed him that, unless he earned his degree from Harvard before the beginning of school, he would forfeit his position. Consequently, instead of preparing to teach his literature classes in the fall, the student devoted his time to completing his philosophy degree. Upon submitting a brilliant and original thesis, he was told that it lacked the necessary scholarly apparatus. His work was provisionally rejected until he could supply the appropriate secondary references. It was only with the utmost difficulty and with the greatest assurances of his academic competence that the student's professors were able to convince the president of the college to allow him to teach that year. The next spring, the student submitted his revised thesis, passed his exams, and received his Ph.D.

For James, this is a quintessential case of the abuse of higher degrees. Far from advancing the scholarship of those involved, the Ph.D. was a great obstacle to it. It is quite obvious that the candidate's instruction in literature must have suffered from the necessary concentration on his dissertation in philosophy. And it is not clear that the candidate's ability to teach literature was in the least improved during the whole process. The whole point of the requirement was so that the college could advertise that all of its instructors possessed the Ph.D. This is a case, James concludes, in which the interests of the individuals—students and instructor alike—were sacrificed for the alleged good of the institution.

James points out that higher degrees were originally established in order to stimulate scholarship, especially original research. Although the degrees themselves are nothing more than "adventitious rewards" (MS, 335), they often spur students on to levels of work that they otherwise would not attain. The sole and valuable purpose of the degrees is the motivation of individuals. But there is a real danger when degrees begin to

> interfere with the free development of talent, to obstruct the natural play of supply and demand in the teaching profession, to foster academic snobbery by the prestige of certain privileged institutions, to transfer accredited value from essential manhood to an outward badge, to blight hopes and promote invidious sentiments, to divert the attention of aspiring youth from direct dealings with the truth to the passing of examinations. (MS, 336)

James singles out for special consideration two specific negative effects of the Ph.D. requirement. First, James calls the refusal to consider for a teaching position applicants who do not have the Ph.D. a case of "pure sham" and "academic snobbery" (MS, 337, 339). The Ph.D. does not in the least guarantee that its possessors will be good teachers. Nor does it guarantee that teachers will be competent in their field of instruction, since often—as in the case of the account with which James begins—they are teaching in a field other than the one in which they earned their Ph.D. The real reason for the requirement, James argues, is to enhance the marketability of the institution. The more Ph.D.s a college can count among its faculty, the more likely it is to attract good students.

A second negative result of the system of higher degrees, James observes, is the damage it does to certain individuals. Some Ph.D. candidates are not sufficiently gifted academically to pass the rigorous requirements for the degree. They are hard workers, often poor, and need the degree to find a teaching position. These students either fail the program and in the process have their spirits broken, or else pity is taken on them and they are passed by a committee whose members acquire bad consciences in the process.

James is further concerned by the fact that once certain titles are well established in a society, it is very difficult to eradicate them. Because he detests the European fashion of allowing titles to make the scholar, he wants his country to be one in which individual merit continues to stand on its own, and not one in which an individual "count[s] for nothing unless stamped and licensed and authenticated by some title-giving machine" (MS, 346–7).

These last points show that James's approval of the university is not without qualification. He realizes the power institutions have and the damage they can inflict on society if that power is abused. For this reason, he wants to make sure that universities—and all other social institutions, as well—are guided by the needs of the individuals constituting them. Institutions guided by this policy can play important roles in facilitating the growth of geniuses and non-geniuses and in stimulating their interaction, both of which James considers to be essential elements of social evolution.

Comparing James's discussion of religious versus academic institutions, we can see he is much harder on the church than on the university. Part of this disparity may be due to anti-ecclesiastical views James inherited from his father, a liberal and independent-minded theologian who broke quite radically with the Calvinism of *his* father. James's father had little time for organized religion and its institution the church. Part of this disparity in James's treatment of the church and the university may also be due to the fact that he wrote about these institutions at different times in his life. In Part II , I will argue that James undergoes a gradual conversion in his thinking between the time of his writings on the church and those on the university. Had he written more about the church after this conversion, he might have had more favorable things to say about it. He might have seen ways in which it, too, could have been a guardian of social evolution. This is a point to which we will return in chapter 4.

For now, it is crucial to note James's general view that, important as institutions can be in the process of social evolution, it is individuals who are at the center of it. Individuals are the ones ultimately responsible for the introduction of novelty, for its selection, and for its assimilation by the traditional. In the next chapter, we will turn to James's psychological study of the individuals who are so central to social evolution. In the individual psyche, we will find a process similar to the social one of the presentation, selection, and assimilation of novelty. This psychological process will take us a dialectical turn deeper into James's individualism.

CHAPTER 2

Internal Dimensions of James's Individualism

In the last chapter we considered the external relations of individuals to other individuals and to social institutions. We saw that James consistently defends the primary importance of individuals in these relations. For James, individuals are both important in their own right and crucial for social evolution. In this chapter, we will find that the emphasis James places on the individual in his discussion of social change is maintained in his analysis of the psychological composition of the individual self. Turning from the external relations of individuals to their internal relations by examining his view of the individual psyche will deepen our understanding of James's individualism, since it is crucial to know not just *how* he defends the individual but also *what sort* of individual he defends.

James begins his study of introspective psychology in the ninth chapter of his *Principles of Psychology*. He points out that most psychology books begin such a study with simple sensations, since their authors hold these sensations to be the building blocks of which higher states of consciousness are composed. But James argues that beginning with simple sensations actually constitutes the abandonment of the empirical method of investigation because simple sensations are products of analysis and are not present, as such, in our experience. James's method, which he holds to be truly empirical, accepts as the first fact for psychology that "thinking of some sort goes on" (PP, 220, italics deleted). James calls this thinking the "stream of thought, of consciousness, or of subjective life" (PP, 233) and presents what he holds to be its five basic, readily observable characteristics. A close analysis of these characteristics will show us the rudiments of the individualism in James's psychology. It will also reveal some of the tensions in that individualism.

THE STREAM OF CONSCIOUSNESS

The first characteristic James mentions is, "Every thought tends to be a part of a personal consciousness" (PP, 220). James observes that introspection reveals sharp divisions between personal thinkers. We have no evidence of thoughts that do not belong to some particular thinker, and it seems that no thought can be experienced by more than one thinker. James writes:

> Each of these minds keeps its own thoughts to itself. There is no giving or bartering between them. No thought even comes into direct *sight* of a thought in another personal consciousness than its own. Absolute insulation, irreducible pluralism, is the law. . . . The breaches between . . . thoughts are the most absolute breaches in nature. . . . The universal conscious fact is not 'feelings and thoughts exist,' but 'I think' and 'I feel.' (PP, 221)

These strong words are softened somewhat in the pages that follow. First, James admits that there may be more than one self in a consciousness. He points out that studies of the subconscious, especially those involving hypnosis, have revealed secondary and even tertiary selves lurking in the depths of some abnormal consciousnesses. But this does not make a significant exception to his thesis, since the thoughts in these consciousnesses tend to be owned by one or another of these selves. A second and more important reason for softening his words about the separation between human consciousnesses is a result of James's interest in the preternatural. He writes: "As for insulation, it would be rash, in view of the phenomena of thought-transference, mesmeric influence and spirit-control, which are being alleged nowadays on better authority than ever before, to be too sure about that point . . ." (PP, 331). These exceptions notwithstanding, it seems correct to say that James holds each individual self to be a stream of consciousness that generally flows singly from its source, not coming into direct contact with any other stream.

The second characteristic of thought James mentions is that, within each stream, "thought is always changing" (PP, 220). Some psychologists believe in the existence of mental atoms. Locke, for example, argues that our mental states are composed of such atoms, which he calls "simple ideas." James is opposed to this atomic view of consciousness. When he writes that thought is in constant change, he means that "no state once gone can recur and be identical with what it was before" (PP, 224). That is, every mental state is unique, leaving no room for identical recurrent atomic states.

The reason we are so strongly tempted to believe in simple ideas, according to James, is that we normally use our perceptions merely to extract from them the conceptions needed to get along in the world. Untrained art students usually rely too much on their conception of what the subject *should* look like and too little on their *actual* perception of it. This is similar to the way we lead our lives from day to day. We are usually far less concerned with our actual subjective sensations than with establishing the identity of some object. James writes, "We hear the same *note* over and over again; we see the same *quality* of green, or smell the same objective perfume, or experience the same *species* of pain" (PP, 225). But our sensations, he points out, are much more complex than that. Our sensation of the green grass in the sunshine is actually very different from that of the green grass in the shade. What we see is conditioned by the visual realities that border it temporally and spatially. Our sensibility to a bright color is diminished if we look at it for a long time. A red looks very different on a green background than on a white or a blue one. Furthermore, James observes, our perceptions are also colored by our subjective conditions. Being tired or hungry or happy affects our perceptions of things. Similar as we conceive our mental states to be, James concludes, the fact that each is different argues against Locke's theory of identical and recurrent simple ideas.

James argues against the existence of simple ideas on physiological grounds, as well. Simple ideas would require identical objects to be perceived in the same way by brains in identical states. Because it is physiologically impossible for a brain to be twice in exactly the same state, there will be a difference, however slight, in the way we experience an object. Thus, for James, physiology concurs with introspection in arguing against the existence of Locke's recurrent simple ideas.

If there are no such things as identical simple ideas, James observes, then it is much less likely that identical complex states exist. Our perception of the world is in constant change. Certain parts of the world are sometimes of great interest to us, while at other times they do not capture our imaginations at all. Certain people seem fascinating for a time and then appear to be completely boring. Beliefs that call out to us as being worthy of all acceptation at some points in our lives often seem later to be totally untenable. At every moment, we are being changed by our experience into something we never were before.

James points out that it is often helpful to think of certain states of mind as identical, just as it is often helpful to treat curves as a series of short, straight lines, or to think of electricity as a fluid. He does not take issue with such useful conceptual formulations, as long as these conceptual symbols are not confused with the percepts themselves. The conceptualization of experience, James argues, must not be conflated with what we are actually perceiving.[1]

A concomitant of Locke's doctrine of simple ideas is Hume's view that, within each thinker, thoughts are discrete and not part of a continuous stream. This view leads to severe problems, such as difficulties in accounting for self-identity. Just as James, with his second characteristic of the stream of consciousness, rejects Locke's doctrine of simple ideas, so with his third characteristic, he opposes Hume's view of the discreteness of mental states.

James's third characteristic of the stream of consciousness is that "within each personal consciousness, thought is sensibly continuous" (PP, 220). That is, although there are unbridged gaps between parallel streams of consciousness, there are no gaps within any particular stream of consciousness. According to James, neither time gaps nor successions of discrete objects of thought are sufficient to break up the stream of consciousness. With felt time-gaps (such as sleep), the consciousnesses on both sides of the gap have a sense of belonging to the same self, and are thus continuous parts of a common whole. We often take the discreteness of conceived objects for the discreteness of their perception. We use language to name the discrete objects of our conception, and then forget that our perceptions do not come in such neat packages. But James argues that a sense of what just happened and an expectation of what is to come, as well as our present bodily condition, always unify the things we experience, so that no perception occurs in total isolation from the rest of the contents of our consciousness. Although it may at first seem that the hearing of thunder at close range causes a definite break in our consciousness, closer analysis shows that the sound of thunder following silence is very different from the sound of thunder following other thunder. James concludes that, even here, our perception is shown to be continuous.

According to James, consciousness does not consist of a series of distinct ideas separated by breaks; rather, it is a stream that includes both substantive and transitive parts. In the substantive parts, the stream moves more slowly, and we perceive things or think thoughts that seem to carry with them more of a sense of permanence. In the transitive states—James's name for relations—the stream moves so quickly that it is almost impossible to carry out an introspective analysis of the movement. For this reason, Hume and other empiricists have claimed that these transitive states do not exist and that what are often thought of as relations are really only gaps between juxtaposed ideas. Intellectualists have defended the existence of these relations, but have relegated them to the realm of pure thought, prior and superior to the objects they relate. James rejects both views. He admits that transitive states are not easy to notice, since they are so fleeting and since our language rarely recognizes them. The difficulty of their perception notwithstanding, James argues that these transitive states are given to us in the flux of experience and that they have feelings associated with them.

James argues further that transitive states are not the only parts of the experiential flux that are difficult to perceive. He maintains that there are other examples of unnamed states of consciousness, as well. It is as though James is here inviting us to look into the shadows of our consciousness and see that they are not all black. Shadows are important, and they come in a variety of different shades. We all know experientially the feeling of trying to remember a particular name. We do not know what the name is, but we are able to reject names we know are not the one we are trying to recall. Sometimes we even know the first letter of the name, how many syllables it has, and what its rhythm is. Feelings of familiarity connected with a certain sound or smell, feelings connected with the verbal skeletons of logical relations, the feeling of intending to say something—all these are feelings of tendency that are often ignored but that, for James, have their place in the stream of consciousness. James's purpose in pointing out these examples is to reinstate "the vague to its proper place in our mental life" (PP, 246).[2]

The fourth basic characteristic of thought James discusses is that it "always appears to deal with objects independent of itself" (PP, 220).[3] James here rejects the Kantian notion that a consciousness of the self is a prerequisite of all knowledge. For James, primitive knowledge involves only a certain consciousness, without the thought that there is a self that somehow owns it. It is through our recognition of sameness in the objects that surround us, he argues, that we come to know that we know; that is, that the self becomes separated from the act of knowing. Through naming similar objects, we come to know that they exist, not only here and now, but also in remote spatiotemporal locations in a way that is accessible to our memories and expectations. Yet James argues that this recognition of sameness is not a prerequisite of all thought. Instead, he holds that, although it often does, thought does not have to make a cognitive distinction between itself and its object.

James also rejects Kant's idea that there is a manifold of discrete and separate ideas in the stream of consciousness that must be synthesized. Although he admits that the objects of our thought are more complex than the words we use to describe them, James argues that the thought of each object is one undivided state of consciousness. He writes, "Whatever things are thought in relation are thought from the outset in a unity, in a single pulse of subjectivity, a single psychosis, feeling, or state of mind" (PP, 268). That is, the complexity of the objects of our thought is revealed to us, not through synthesis, but through analysis.

The final basic characteristic James mentions is that thought is selective with respect to the independent objects it considers. He writes, "It is interested in some parts of these objects to the exclusion of others, and welcomes or rejects—*chooses* from among them, in a word—all the while" (PP, 220). Selection, James points out, occurs at every level of consciousness—in sensation, perception, empirical experience, reasoning, aesthetics, and ethics. Our sense organs pick up only certain types of facts. Our eyes, for example, sense light of only a small range of wavelengths; our ears, sounds of only a small range of pitches. Of our sensations, attention picks out certain ones as interesting and ignores the rest. We divide the world into things and perceive the reality of these things to be signified by sensations that are usually absent. Empirical thought depends on things we have experienced, and our experiences are largely determined by our habits of attending to what is of interest to us. Reasoning depends on the ability of the mind to break up the totality of the phenomenon reasoned about into parts and to pick out from among these the particular one that leads to the proper conclusion. Aesthetics is obviously about selection, as is ethics; the production of a work of art involves selection of both subject and style, and an action has no ethical quality whatever unless it is chosen from more than one possible action.

Pervasive as James takes selection to be, it is not surprising that it takes on two different meanings in his writings. First, selection is a kind of action. From several possibilities, we actively choose one and exclude the others. Second, selection stands for that which is selected, especially in the cognitive realm. In this sense, conceptions are selections, since they are cognitive structures created by focusing on certain perceptual realities and ignoring the rest.

It is important to note here that the pervasiveness of selection in James's thought is not without its balancing characteristics, which he has already presented. There is a significant contrast between James's second and third characteristics of thought, on the one hand, and his fifth characteristic, on the other. The contrast is between the vague and mercurial continuity of thought on the one hand and its ordering and stabilization through selection on the other. A central problem in James's thought is the tension between remaining true to the Heraclitean and highly nuanced world of perception and valuing the freedom and the practical benefits that come with the ability to select.

James is deeply committed to the task of remaining true to the perceptual world of concrete experience. The success of painters, novelists, musicians, and wine-tasters is due in large part to their sensitivity to their perceptions and their ability to make us more sensitive to our own. In refusing to yield to the temptation to lump similar things together and then to forget that they are not identical, these artists are able to show us that there are different colors of shadows, different levels of anger, different ways of hearing middle C, and different kinds of fruity wine. Artists, however, are not the only ones for whom perceptual sensitivity is important. James's interest and success in psychology, for example, are due, in large part, to his sensitivity to his own psychological functions.

Going beyond perception, James also understands the value of selection. At the end of this chapter, we will see that James holds selection to be the essence of volition, and thus of the freedom that is a prerequisite for meaning. He also holds that selection is essential for conceptualization.

This tension between reception and perception on the one hand and selection and conception on the other is centrally important for our study of James's individualism. It raises the question whether James's individual is chiefly a receptive perceiver, or chiefly a selective conceiver? We will take up this question in chapter 4. In chapter 5, we will see how, in his writings on perception and conception in the last years of his life, James finally finds a way to lessen the tension between his loyalty to concrete experience and his appreciation of the value of selection.

Having presented the five basic characteristics of thought, James turns from a discussion of thought in general to its specific role in human consciousness. In accordance with the first general characteristic of thought, that every thought tends to be a part of a personal consciousness, James takes up the task of examining the personal consciousness to which thought tends to belong.

THE CONSCIOUSNESS OF SELF

James divides the constituents of personal consciousness into two classes: the empirical self and the pure ego. The empirical self includes the material self, the social self, and the spiritual self. The material self, in turn, consists of our body, clothes, family, home, and other physical possessions. By contrast, our social self is the reputation we have with our friends, colleagues, and others. Finally, our spiritual self is most central to whom we feel ourselves to be. Taken concretely, it is the entire stream of our consciousness. Taken abstractly, it is our psychic faculties and dispositions, the most important of which are perception, conception, and volition. The bulk of *Principles* is dedicated to an analysis of this spiritual self, abstractly taken. Consequently, our discussion of James's psychology will focus mostly on his abstract analysis of the spiritual self. Before I turn to this analysis, however, I want to complete James's picture of the personal consciousness by sketching briefly his understanding of the pure ego.

James begins with a critique of two traditional and contrary ways of understanding the pure ego. Traditional empiricists argue that the self is nothing more than the impressions and ideas it thinks, bundled together in certain ways. By contrast, traditional rationalists, whom James here calls substantialists, claim that the only way to explain the unity of the self is to postulate the existence of the soul, of a simple, immortal substance that does not change through time. James sides with the substantialists in claiming that the empiricist view is insufficient for explaining the unity of consciousness. But he argues that substantialists go too far in their descriptions of this principle of unity. Whatever the advantages of belief in the soul, it also has its disadvantages, and James argues that the empirical facts of psychology can be explained without it. For the purposes of his present investigation, James leaves the soul to one side and presents, instead, his own view of the pure ego and its function as a principle of unification.

James likens thoughts to cattle in a herd. Each of us recognizes our own thoughts because they carry our "brand." This brand is the warmth and continuity that cause us to identify thoughts that have them as ours, and our thoughts carry this brand because they belong, or once belonged, to us. But who is the "me" to which these thoughts belong? James argues that it is the judging pulse in the stream of consciousness that owns them. But this pulse is not the never-changing soul of the substantialists. Rather, it is a Thought that plays the role of the rancher who owns the herd of thoughts. But unlike a human rancher, the Thought never lasts for more than a moment. When it comes into being, it inherits the thoughts that belonged to the Thought it succeeds, adds to them the new thoughts it experiences, then passes away, willing its entire herd of thoughts to the Thought that succeeds it.

This brief sketch of James's theory of the pure ego is sufficient for present purposes. There is no need for us to take it up in more detail or to assess its strength.[4] Instead, it will be of more value to our study to return to James's examination of the spiritual self.

It must be remembered that James's treatment of the spiritual self in *Principles* is, for the most part, abstract. The spiritual self as we actually experience it concretely, James notes, always involves a variety of psychological faculties working simultaneously. For the purposes of psychological analysis, however, James isolates the various faculties, discussing each in turn.

Although James is not as explicit about this as he might have been, his abstract analysis of the spiritual self in *Principles* is based on the reflex action model of the self. Consequently, it will be important to understand this model and how James applies it psychologically before we delve into the details of his discussion in *Principles*. James discusses the reflex action model of the self in "Reflex Action and Theism," an address he delivered in 1881 and the text of which was eventually included in *Will to Believe* (WB, 90–113). Taking up this address first will help us understand the model underlying James's discussion of the individual self in *Principles* and will, at the same time, provide us with an outline for proceeding through that discussion.

THE REFLEX ACTION MODEL OF THE SELF

James's main point in "Reflex Action and Theism" is that the reflex structure of the self naturally tends toward theism. This thesis, which James himself later admits to have been weakly supported,[5] need not concern us here. More important is James's description of the triadic structure of the self. He maintains that the self consists of three main "departments": perception, conception, and volition. James's description of these departments is not very precise, but he does give us a general sense of the kinds of processes he subsumes under each.

The first department consists of sensation and perception. It is the way in which we come in contact with what we call the "facts of nature." It is largely a receptive process whose function is to get an impression from an object it confronts. The second department includes the processes of conception, reflection, theorizing, and thinking in general. This department is responsible for defining the object sensed in the first department. The third department is controlled by our volitional nature, which consists of our "definite subjective purposes, preferences, fondnesses for certain effects, forms, orders" (WB, 95). As a place of reaction in accordance with our desires, its function is to decide what active measures an object's presence demands.

The reflex action model of the self suggests not only a triadic division of the self, but also a particular relation among its three departments. James writes, "The sensory impression exists only for the sake of awakening the central process of reflection, and the central process of reflection exists only for the sake of calling forth the final act" (WB, 92). This emphasis on the third department as the final goal of the other two shows the reflex action model to be essentially a "teleological mechanism" (WB, 94). It is the means by which we transform our world in accordance with the desires of our volitional natures. Conception occupies a peculiar place between perception and volition. It is dependent on perception for its premises, and its conclusions are not complete unless they represent volitional discharges in department three that have some real effect in the world. In James's own words,

> [T]he middle stage of consideration or contemplation or thinking is only a place of transit, the bottom of a loop, both whose ends have their point of application in the outer world. If it should ever have no roots in the outer world, if it should ever happen that it led to no active measures, it would fail of its essential function, and would have to be considered either pathological or abortive. (WB, 92)[6]

Keeping in mind that James bases his understanding of the spiritual self on the reflex action model, we can now see that the second volume of his *Principles* is dedicated to the explication of the details of this connection. Chapters XVII–XXI explore the first department in their discussions of sensation, imagination, and perception. Chapter XXII, entitled "Reasoning," deals with the second department. And chapters XXIII–XXVI lay out the components of the third department in their discussions of the production of movement, instinct, emotion, and the will. A closer look at the content of these chapters will show us more clearly James's psychological doctrine of the self and give us insight into his notion of the internal relations of the individual.[7]

Perception

Suppose I want to cross a street. I look both ways and see a car coming from the left. I wait until the car passes, then walk across. This common experience is not composed of mere sensations. My senses report only that a red object in a certain part of my field of vision is becoming larger and that a particular purring sound is becoming louder. This sensory experience is associated with other experiences I have had, so that I am able to perceive the danger of an approaching car. James argues that, although sensation and perception are not independent components of such an experience, they can be abstracted out of the experience.[8] As long as we keep in mind that sensation and perception are not, for James, discrete building blocks of experience, it will be instructive to examine what he holds to be their respective contributions to it.

James argues that sensation is temporally prior to perception and to all other psychological functions, as well. In fact, he claims that consciousness begins with sensation. In his view, before sensation there are only nerve currents in the brain, but with sensation comes consciousness. A pure sensation is a consciousness of the unmodified data supplied by the senses. Because of the structure of our brains, pure sensation can occur only in the first few weeks of life. These first impressions leave copies that are stored in the brain and can be called up again in the imagination after the actual impressions are gone. Subsequent impressions call up these copies through association; thus, our actual experience is informed, not only through sensation, but also through perception, which involves the related images in the brain. The older we get, James continues, the more copies we have stored in our brain, and the richer the associative connections to any particular experience we may have.

Thus, James holds that both sensations and perceptions contribute to our experience and that the only way to separate their contributions is through abstraction. On the concrete level, he maintains, they are joined at the preconscious level in such a way that they form a single conscious experience that is different from what either would produce alone.[9]

Reason

Consider what we normally term reflex responses. A doctor strikes my knee with his rubber mallet, and my knee jerks. An object rapidly approaches my eye, and it closes quickly. These are cases where information from my senses triggers an automatic response over which I have no control. Nerve currents arriving from the periphery trigger messages to the stimulated areas without awakening consciousness. In these cases, we know our behavior, not from a sense of having willed it, but by observing it as it occurs. Prior to our behavior, we have no clearer idea of what it will be than does a bystander. According to James, this is analogous to instinctual behavior in animals. Animals often behave without deliberation in ways triggered by stimuli in their environment. Instinctual behavior admits of no rational interlude at the nexus between data and action. There is no reflection at the flexion point.

In higher animals, including human beings, James notes, there are also other types of behavior that can result from various types of thinking. Empirical thinking, as defined by James, occurs when concrete thoughts are linked together through similarity and contiguity (as happens in our experience of reverie). They may stop when no further images are called up by a particular image, or they may remind us of some practical task we must accomplish.

More similar to reasoning, according to James, are the "unconscious inferences" we make in associating incoming data with information already in our minds. Sometimes, as in the case of perception, this occurs below the level of consciousness. The datum is a sign that refers to a "recept." A recept is a notion of a general object that forms the basis of our action. The association between sign and recept occurs on the basis of continual association of the two in the past. A few years after the publication of *Principles*, Pavlov's famous dogs practiced such unconscious inferences when they salivated at the sound of the bell. Because of repeated experience, the dogs had associated the sign (the bell) with the recept (the idea of food). It was on the basis of this association that, even when the food was absent, the dogs unconsciously reacted by salivating. Of course, this reaction on the basis of unconscious influences was completely dependent on past experience. According to James, only full-fledged reasoning will work in dealing with novel situations.

While unconscious inferences are applications of unprocessed associations learned in the past, James understands reasoning to be what I will call "essential thinking." Reasoning, for James, consists of the perception and processing of essences by means of sagacity and learning. In order to understand James's essential thinking, we have to be clear about what these terms mean. Most important, we have to be clear about what James means by "essence."

Philosophers have traditionally distinguished between a thing's essence and its attributes. A thing's essence is unchanging; it is what the thing *really is*, and it cannot be directly sensed by an observer. A thing's attributes consist of qualities such as color, smell, and texture—changeable qualities that can be sensed by the observer. James rejects this view and returns essences to experience. A thing's essence, he argues, is one of its perceivable attributes and not something that stands behind the attributes. Because of our analytical abilities, we are able to break up an object into various perceivable attributes and then abstract a particular one, the thing's essence, from the others. But what sets off the essential attribute from the non-essential ones? For James, the essential attribute is the one that has a teleological connection with the role the thing is to play within a certain context. Since it is contextual, a thing's essence varies, depending on the use to which the thing is to be put. James writes, "The essence of a thing is that one of its properties which is so *important for my interests* that in comparison with it I may neglect the rest" (PP, 961).

James illustrates his point by referring to a piece of paper. In the process of writing, the paper's essential attribute is that of a surface for inscription. But if the goal is to light a fire, its essential property is clearly its combustibility. In other situations, other attributes—its thinness, its hydrocarbonous composition, its size, its position, or its origin—might become essential. To argue that paper must always essentially be "paper" because that is what everyone calls it is to fail to realize that a thing's popular name is merely one of its aspects that is useful in certain situations and not in others. The same is true of its chemical composition. A chemical analysis, James maintains, does not tell us what the thing "really" is, except in the context of certain scientific purposes.

James's view provides an answer to Sir Arthur Eddington's dilemma about whether to accept the phenomenological table or the scientific table as real. According to James, the phenomenological table is real for phenomenological purposes, and the scientific table is real for scientific purposes. He argues that we cannot go beyond this pragmatic solution. For him, there is no such thing as an absolute and immutable essence existing in eternal contradistinction to the uses to which a thing is to be put. An essence is not a purely intellectual quality of a thing. Nor is it something that belongs exclusively either to the subject or to the object. Instead, an essence, for James, is a function of context, of the relation between subject and object.

It is crucial that James's notion of essence be understood to be contextual and neither exclusively subjective nor exclusively objective. The view that essences are exclusively objective is at the root of the scientism James fights against so strongly in *The Will to Believe* and elsewhere. A belief that scientific investigation yields the infallible and immutable truth about our world is only a small step away from believing, with W. K. Clifford, that it is immoral to believe something on any but "scientific" grounds. In philosophy and religion, the view that essences are exclusively objective is an example of the "over-simplification" James identifies as the "root of all that absolutism and one-sided dogmatism by which both philosophy and religion have been infested" (VRE, 30). Thus, in science, philosophy, and religion, James holds that the view that essences are objective leads to tyranny.

The view that essences are exclusively subjective is just as dangerous. It leads not to tyranny, but to anarchy. If there are no external limitations to what a person may legitimately view as a thing's essence, then there seems little basis for interpersonal communication, education, and morality. If essences are subjectively determined, it is hard to see how any social function that involves the critique of one person's thinking by another can be considered legitimate.

James himself makes statements that, at times, seem to support such subjectivity. He writes, for example, "All ways of conceiving a concrete fact, if they are true ways at all, are equally true ways. There is no property absolutely essential to any one thing" (PP, 959, italics and capitals deleted). Yet a careful reading shows that James both attacks objectivism and stops short of subjectivism. To see this clearly, we must look in more detail at James's analysis of the reasoning process.

James sees reasoning as syllogistic, its purpose being to find a middle term that leads from present data to a desired end. Consider the syllogism:

$$M \text{ is } P.$$
$$\underline{S \text{ is } M.}$$
$$\therefore S \text{ is } P.$$

S stands for the fact or concrete datum, M stands for the essential attribute, and P stands for the essential property's desired consequence. If M is, indeed, an attribute of S, if M leads to P, and if P is the goal, then this thinking is correct. If, on the other hand, N is selected as the middle term and N leads not to P but to Q, the reasoner who selected N as the essence of S is thinking incorrectly. Of course, if Q is the desired end, then the thinker who takes M to be the essence of S is mistaken.

An example will help to clarify what James means by syllogistic thinking. Suppose that data have been collected on women who have tested positive on GenTest 1000, a cheap, over-the-counter genetic test, and that these data are being examined by a doctor and a sociologist. Suppose, further, that the doctor's goal is to identify those women who are at risk for developing breast cancer. Given this goal, the doctor is quite right to take the essence of a positive result on the test to be the presence of $BRCA_1$, a gene linked to the development of breast cancer. Suppose, on the other hand, that the sociologist's goal is to test a hypothesis regarding the link between socioeconomic status and belief in the value of genetic testing. Given this goal, the sociologist is quite right to take the essence of a positive result on the test to be an indication of a belief in the value of genetic testing.

On James's view, the doctor and the sociologist have both correctly identified the essence of the meaning of the data *for their specific purposes*. If the doctor had identified the essence of the data to be a determination of belief in the value of genetic testing and the sociologist had identified it to be an indication of a likelihood of developing breast cancer, both would have been mistaken. Thus, James's view that a thing's essence is relative to its context does not force him into a subjectivism in which reasoning is a completely private affair. Although reasoning is held to be a tool of subjective desires, it can be mistaken in a way that is objectively apparent.[10]

Given that essences are context-dependent, James names sagacity as the means we use to identify them. That is, sagacity is the ability to choose the one attribute of a thing that is important for our ends. James maintains that sagacity is guided by our practical and aesthetic interests. Thus, the greater our interests and needs, the greater our need for reasoning.

James identifies association by similarity as one of the most important tools sagacity uses to identify essences. It is often very difficult to determine a thing's essence. In a particular situation, a thing S possesses so many attributes that it is difficult to ignore all but the correct one M. In such cases, it is often helpful to consider things that are similar to S. By holding S, S', and S" in our minds at the same time, it often happens that the attribute M common to them all is much easier to identify.[11]

James further argues that sagacity, which allows us to perceive a thing's essence, must be supplemented by learning to complete the reasoning process. Learning is the method by which we process the thing's essence, showing to what useful conclusion it leads. Learning involves a knowledge of the various consequences and concomitants of essences. In the standard syllogism, sagacity is required for the minor premise, and learning for the major premise.

James claims that syllogistic reasoning is a powerful way of arriving at a desired end because a thing's essence points to a particular consequence more clearly than does the thing itself. He supports his claim with two arguments. First, an essence is more familiar to us than the thing for which it stands. Because it is more general, it belongs to a variety of things in our experience. Thus, we are more familiar with it than with any of the particular things in which it occurs. Second, an essence has fewer properties than the thing for which it stands, so it is easier to see the consequences to which it leads.

Action

Having explored the first two faculties of perception and reasoning, James proceeds to consider the third faculty of action. Recalling the teleological structure of the reflex theory, James reminds us that the final result of the inward processes of perception and reasoning is some sort of bodily activity. He writes, "The whole neural organism . . . is, physiologically considered, but a machine for converting stimuli into reactions" (PP, 994). He then discusses in detail the most important of these reactions: instinctive or impulsive performances, expressions of emotion, and voluntary deeds.

James argues that every incoming impression produces some outgoing neural discharge, although we may not be aware of it. The discharge may be so slight that we do not notice it, or its overall effect may be to inhibit some action, thus making it difficult to identify as a positive reaction to stimuli. James further argues that a "process set up anywhere in the [nerve centers] reverberates everywhere, and in some way or other affects the organism throughout, making its activities either greater or less" (PP, 1002, italics deleted). He likens the nerve centers to a good conductor charged with electricity. The tension cannot be changed anywhere on the conductor without changing it everywhere at once.

Instinct

James accepts the traditional definition of instinct as "the faculty of acting in such a way as to produce certain ends, without foresight of the ends, and without previous education in the performance" (PP, 1004, italics deleted). But he does not accept the naming of particular instincts by the abstract purposes they serve. To say that an animal that instinctually preserves its life or lays eggs has an instinct of self-preservation or an instinct of maternity is to credit the animal with obedience to an abstraction that, James holds, it cannot have framed. He argues, instead, that instincts should be understood physiologically as following the general reflex type. Certain sensory stimuli in an animal's environment call forth a particular response, not for the attainment of certain abstract ends, but simply because the animal can act in no other way. A cat, for example, chases mice, runs from dogs, avoids falling from high places, and shuns fire and water, not because it has any notion of life or its preservation, but simply because this is the way it is programmed to act.

James points out that it is common to distinguish animal behavior from human behavior by saying that animal behavior is governed by instinct, whereas human behavior is governed by reason. Yet he argues that there is no essential difference between animal instincts and human impulses such as "blushing, sneezing, coughing, smiling, or dodging, or keeping time to music" (PP, 1006). Because the physiological processes are identical, their difference is only verbal. Thus, human behavior, like animal behavior, is really governed by instinct. Yet this conclusion seems to be palpably out of line with our experience. Animal behavior is obviously instinctual, but human behavior is deliberative. By taking a closer look at how instincts influence behavior, we will be able to see how well James's view actually does correspond to experience.

When we think of instinctual behavior, we usually think of one of the lower animals, whose behavior is governed by a single predominant instinct. We think, for example, of a bird building a nest or sitting on a nest full of eggs. One reason it is difficult to recognize human behavior as instinctual, James argues, is not that human beings have no instincts, but that we have so many of them that they inhibit each other. Our behavior is more finely balanced, more sensitive to subtle changes in the environment, and thus less predictable than animal behavior.

James points out a further complication that tends to mask the instinctive nature of our behavior, as well as that of the higher animals. He argues that our instinctive actions are "blind" only the first time we carry them out. Just as the memory of previous sensations influences our perception of subsequent ones, making it impossible for us to have pure sensations for long, so our memories of previous instinctual behavior influence subsequent behavior and make it impossible to follow instincts blindly for an extended period.

According to James, human behavior cannot, strictly speaking, be deliberative, since only impulses and not reason, per se, are active. Reason is merely capable of exciting the imagination by means of an inference. The imagination thus excited may then give rise to a particular impulse whose behavioral result may be either positive or inhibitive. Thus, although human behavior seems to differ from animal behavior in being deliberative, James concludes that this deliberative appearance is caused, not by a rational principle of action, but by the complex interaction of competing instincts and the memories we have of past experiences of similar instinctual action.

James mentions two other principles of non-uniformity of instincts that may further mask their behavioral influence. First is the law of inhibition of instincts by habits: "When objects of a certain class elicit from an animal a certain sort of reaction, it often happens that the animal becomes partial to the first specimen of the class on which it has reacted, and will not afterward react on any other specimen" (PP, 1014, italics deleted). Our impulses are satisfied by our spouses, our friends, and our diet, so that, once married, once befriended, once in a certain dietary habit, we are no longer led by these impulses to look elsewhere for their satisfaction. Another example of the inhibition of instincts by habits occurs when we have contradictory impulses toward the same object. Once one of these impulses is established, it may suppress its competitor. James uses the example of the opposite impulses of fearing and fondling that animals awaken in children. If in their first encounter with dogs, children are snapped at or bitten, their fondling impulse may be inhibited for years.

The second principle of instincts that can mask their behavioral influence is the law of transitoriness. According to this law, many "instincts ripen at a certain age and then fade away" (PP, 1017, italics deleted). Some instincts are, of course, more transient than others. With the more transient ones, it often happens that, if the right objects are met with while these instincts are vivacious, habits of acting on them are formed—habits that remain even after the instincts have passed away. But if the right objects are not encountered and no such habits form, these objects will not elicit a reaction when they are encountered later in life. As an example of the law of transitoriness, James cites the sucking instinct in human infants. If permitted to do so, babies are content to breast-feed far longer than normal. But infants who are fed with a spoon in the first days of life may never suck at all.

Emotion

James is not content with traditional psychological accounts of emotion, as they consist of little more than descriptive inventories of human emotions. By contrast, he is interested in the causal explanation of emotions, something that is of greater value for science.

We usually think of emotions as being generated directly by objects in our environment. Once our emotions are produced, they, in turn, prompt us to act in certain ways. On this commonsense view, emotions belong with sensation and perception, since they are caused by the environment and precede physical adjustments. The fact that

James includes emotions, not under perception, but under action, shows that he has a very different understanding of emotions. For James, emotions are the conscious concomitants of bodily movements. His view has come to be known as the James–Lange theory of emotions, named in honor of James and Carl G. Lange, a Danish psychologist who developed essentially the same theory concurrently and independently of James.

According to the James–Lange theory of emotions, an object directly excites certain physical changes in our bodies, and our emotions are nothing other than our conscious awareness of these changes. An example will help to make clear the differences between the commonsense view and the view James espouses. Suppose I am walking alone in the woods at night and hear the howl of a wolf. When I hear this sound, I stop dead in my tracks. My heart starts pounding; my breath comes quickly. My hair stands on end; a shiver goes down my spine. I break out in a cold sweat. According to the common view, the wolf's howl made me afraid, and it is my fear that causes these physical effects. James's view, on the other hand, is that my fear is nothing other than the effects in my consciousness of all these physical reactions to the stimulus. I may also experience an instinctive impulse to run. If I give in to this impulse, my physical state again changes, and my fear increases.

Evidence for James's view is largely introspective. Since the honing of introspective skills is not greatly encouraged in our society, it is no wonder that its results are not reflected in the common view of the genesis of emotions. For James, it is important to realize that all bodily movements, whether external or visceral, are felt, even if only very faintly. Our emotions, according to James, are constituted by nothing other than these feelings. To prove this, James suggests that we begin with a strong emotion and then abstract away from it all of its bodily symptoms. If we are careful in our introspection, he predicts, we will find nothing remaining at the end of the process.

If James's view is correct, it would follow that an excitation of the physical movements of which fear is a conscious concomitant, even in the absence of some frightening stimulus, would make us feel fear. James points out that this is precisely what occurs in cases of pathological attacks of fear. He argues that the best way to treat these cases is to address the physical symptoms. Upon the slowing of the heart rate and the breathing, the fear begins to dissipate. James observes that this pattern is also present in actors. By going through the motions of being afraid, they actually experience the emotion of fear. Some actors, it is true, claim that they do not actually feel the emotions they are acting. James hypothesizes that this is due to the difference between the external and the visceral components of the movements that cause emotion. If the visceral components are much more important, going through the external movements while blocking the internal ones would result in little emotion. James asserts, however, that actors who suppress visceral movements do not act as well as their colleagues who do not block them and thus actually feel the emotion.

The distinction between internal and external movement associated with emotion is important for answering another objection to James's theory. It might be claimed that stifling the bodily movements associated with an emotion actually intensifies the emotion. If I get the urge to laugh in church, for example, it seems that the very necessity of keeping a straight face intensifies the impulse to laugh. If I am angry, but am fearful of expressing my anger, it will likely turn into a much stronger hatred. James's answer to this objection is to point out that stifling the external movements, as in the case of laughter, may intensify the internal ones, thus intensifying the emotion, as well. He argues, further, that stifled movements are different from freely expressed ones and result in different emotions. Pent-up anger, for example, involves quite different movements and is thus a very different emotion than explosive anger.

In James's view, it is sometimes difficult to distinguish between emotions and instincts. For James, an instinct never occurs without an emotion. Both involve physical reactions to a stimulating object. Furthermore, these reactions are, in both cases, of the reflex type. We have already discussed instincts as reflex types. James understands emotion to be the sum of various reflex actions. Just as in perception, sensations combine at the preconscious level with images from previous experiences to form one single, seamless perception, so various reflex responses in the body combine at the preconscious level to form one emotion. Because of the great number of possible reflexes and the even greater number of their possible combination, James maintains, we are capable of experiencing both a wide range of emotions and subtle differences between similar emotions.

The main difference, for James, between emotion and instinct is that an emotional reaction usually terminates in one's own body, whereas an instinctive reaction engages the stimulating object through its actions. If I come face to face with the howling wolf in the woods at night, my emotional response consists in palpitation, an increased breathing rate, and sweaty palms, whereas my instinctive response is "fight or flight."

Given that emotion involves internal responses to stimuli, why do we experience these physiological responses at all? Why do I respond to the howl of a wolf with an increased heart and breathing rate, a cold sweat, and a dry mouth? James mentions two principles that have been advanced to explain our physical responses. First is the principle of "revival in weakened form of reactions useful in more violent dealings with the object inspiring the emotion" (PP, 1092, italics deleted). According to this principle, physical responses are weakened repetitions of former useful movements or their concomitants. Fear, for example, is explained as the presence, in a slight degree, of the very movements of fight or flight that we would experience if we were actually attacked. The increased breathing rate is said to be due to "organic reminiscences" of heavy breathing during a fight or panting during flight. Second is the principle of "reacting similarly to analogous-feeling stimuli" (PP, 1094, italics deleted). According to this principle, emotional reactions are caused by our tendency to respond similarly in situations in which we experience analogous stimulation. For example, when babies do not want to eat something they are being fed, they move their heads from side to side to avoid taking the disagreeable food into their mouths. According to this principle, adults generalize this response and apply it analogically to any distasteful idea. When babies want to eat the food, on the other hand, they nod forward to put it into their mouths. Analogically, the principle explains, adults nod as an expression of assent.

Some emotional responses, James observes, are as yet inexplicable and must be accepted as idiopathic. Of these, some are actually pathological and others seem to be accidental results of the complexity of our systems. James identifies symptoms of terror, which are actually harmful to the person experiencing them, as examples of the former, and aesthetic emotions, which, he contends, could not have developed for the sake of utility, as examples of the latter.

Will

James maintains that instinctual and emotional movements are primary. He means by this that they are movements that, in accordance with the neural structure of the organism, automatically follow certain stimuli. In animals without memory, these movements are always produced without a prevision of the results, with the animal becoming aware of the results only because of the action. In animals with memory, these movements are produced without a prevision of the results only the first time they are performed. Thereafter, the animal has a memory of the movement and knows what ends it is likely to produce. It is this very memory, and the knowledge to which it gives rise, James argues, that makes voluntary action possible.

Voluntary movements, for James, are secondary. If we have a certain end in mind, we must turn to the memories of our past involuntary actions to see which actions are possible. From this supply of actions, first performed involuntarily, we select the movement that seems most appropriate to achieving the desired end. The motor-cue, or the idea of movement, that immediately precedes voluntary movements is an anticipation of the movement's sensible effects. Sometimes, especially when just learning to perform a complicated action, we anticipate each movement that the various parts of our body must make. With actions with which we are more familiar, the motor-cue may merely be an anticipation of the final result of the action. James argues that the motor-cue is all that is necessary to select what kind of action is to be performed. Sometimes, he continues, this selection is sufficient to cause an action to be performed; sometimes an extra effort of the will is needed. When the motor-cue is sufficient to produce the action, it is called ideomotor action; when extra effort is required, it is called deliberative action.

Because nondeliberative, ideomotor action is simpler, James takes it as the fundamental type of the process of volition. Ideomotor action occurs when a movement follows the bare thought of it. When something fragile slips from our hands, for example, and we quickly reach down to catch it before it shatters on the floor, we are performing ideomotor action. In such cases, we are unable to distinguish between the conception and the execution of the action in question. Ideomotor action is possible, James argues, because consciousness is naturally impulsive. The overall structure of our being, following the general reflex-type, is such that the neural currents generated by sensations and modified by thoughts have movements as their natural consequence.

Sometimes, James observes, a particular movement does not follow its idea because it is blocked by an idea of a contrary movement. This initiates the process of deliberative action. We are first thrown into a state of indecision, an inward feeling of unrest. So long as the contrary objects are in our minds, we are in a state of deliberation and unable to act. Deliberation is ended by a decision involving the triumph of one of the objects and the defeat of the others. When the alarm clock goes off in the morning, we may experience an impulse to get up immediately. If we follow this impulse, we are engaging in ideomotor action. It may be, however, that our impulse to get up is blocked by the idea of staying in bed and going back to sleep. When this happens, we go into a state of indecision, unsure whether to get up or to go back to sleep. This state of indecision persists until either the impulse to get up, often fueled by guilt or by expectation, is triumphant or the idea of going back to sleep lulls us into somnolence.

James describes five main types of decision-making common in ending the state of indecision. First is the reasonable type, where the reasons for and against a certain action almost seem to work themselves out and leave a clear indication of which possible action should be followed. This type of decision-making is usually effected, James says, by finding a way of classifying the problem so that it fits under some rule of action that we have already adopted. Just as in reasoning, so in acting, the important thing seems to be to find the correct way of conceiving the situation. If we are able to define the problem in accord with some decision-making principle, indecision will soon end.

The second and third types of decision-making James describes are similar to each other. In both cases, the decision is made before all the evidence is in. The alternatives we are contemplating both seem good, and the most important thing is to make some kind of decision. In the second type of decision, we take action in accordance with some external suggestion, such as what others are doing or what they expect of us. In the third type of decision, we take action in accordance with some internal suggestion, often without really knowing why we are deciding to act in a certain way. Once we start acting, James says, the relief in having made some type of decision often animates us and makes us think that the chosen course of action is, indeed, the correct one.

The fourth type of decision-making involves a change of heart. We are able to make a decision because our point of view undergoes a radical change. For example, we may encounter a very strong reminder of our mortality and, as a consequence, experience a change from a lighthearted mood to a very serious one in which all courses of action but one suddenly seem totally inappropriate.

The fifth type of decision-making is carried out through effort. In the previous four types, whatever effort there may have been during deliberation comes to an end once a decision has been made. All other possible actions fall away, and we act in accordance with the only one left. In this final type, however, we must expend effort even in carrying out the action on which we have decided. The other possible actions are still in our minds, and we are very much aware that, by acting in the way we have decided to act, we are choosing against the possibilities they represent. Whether or not we believe that our decision is clearly the most rational one given the evidence, its execution requires effort.

This feeling of effort is centrally important for James's psychology of the will. Although the phenomenological experience of effort is not a matter of debate, James argues, its interpretation is.[12] Since James's explanation of free will is closely tied to his understanding of the exertion of effort, it behooves us to examine the latter more closely.

According to James, different mental objects carry with them different strengths of impulses to act. He writes that, for most people, the more powerful mental objects tend to include objects of passion, appetite, or emotion; feelings or ideas of pleasure or pain; objects to which we have developed a habitual reaction; and ideas relatively near in space and time. Less powerful objects are usually highly abstract conceptions, unaccustomed reasons, and those that are contrary to the instincts we have developed in our evolutionary history. The triumph of one mental object over the others in a particular situation results from a number of complex factors, including the character and current disposition of the person in question. Normally, James observes, it is the stronger, more concrete ideas that win out over the weaker, more abstract ones and that go on to produce the action. But it is possible to reinforce the weaker objects by means of effort so that they are able to overpower their naturally stronger competitors. To see how James believes strong ideas can be overpowered through mental effort, we must turn for a moment to his discussion of attention (see PP, chapter XI).

According to James, there are two types of attention: voluntary and involuntary. Involuntary attention occurs when our minds follow the thoughts they find most interesting. In daydreaming, for example, we let our minds wander effortlessly from one image to the next, in accordance with natural associations. If, however, our daydreaming occurs when we are supposed to be listening to a lecture, we may try to exercise voluntary attention. This means going against the natural flow of our thinking to focus on one particular thought that would normally be crowded out by its fellows. James claims that voluntary attention cannot last for more than a few seconds. If the lecture does not capture our involuntary attention, we will begin to daydream again after a few seconds. If our involuntary attention is never engaged, we will be able to attend to the lecture only by a series of repeated, brief efforts of voluntary attention.

James takes geniuses to be people who are capable of an unusual amount of sustained attention. It would be natural to suppose that they are capable of such sustained attention by virtue of an unusually strong will that brings their mind back to the topic at hand whenever it starts to wander. But James argues that, in most geniuses, sustained attention is not voluntary, but involuntary. Geniuses have such fresh and original minds that topics from which normal minds would wander out of sheer boredom can hold their attention for hours. This is because geniuses are able to see more interesting and detailed divisions and connections in a particular topic than most are able to see. James writes that "it is their genius making them attentive, not their attention making geniuses of them" (PP, 400, italics deleted). According to James, the daydreams of an ordinary person and the contemplations of a genius resemble each other in that they are both involuntary. They differ from each other only in the objects on which this involuntary attention is focused. Ordinary daydreams flit about from topic to topic, whereas the thoughts of geniuses revolve around a single topic.

Important as geniuses are, James points out that they also have their weaknesses. He writes that "the faculty of voluntarily bringing back a wandering attention, over and over again, is the very root of judgment, character, and will" (PP, 401). Because geniuses have less of a need to exercise their voluntary attention, they are less likely than non-geniuses to have exemplary moral virtues developed by a strong will.

We are now in a position to see the importance of James's discussion of attention for his view of the will. Volition, for James, is really nothing other than voluntary attention. He writes, "Effort of attention is . . . the essential phenomenon of will" (PP, 1167, italics deleted). One consequence of this is the distinction between volition and physical action. Once an action is willed, James maintains, it passes out of the psychology of the will and into the physiology of movement. The movement then either follows or does not follow, depending on physiological conditions inside the body and physical conditions outside the body. Thus, for James, the question of whether the movement is actually performed is separate from the question of whether it was willed. He finds the process of willing to be of more interest, and it is this process on which I will focus here.

James argues that, assuming favorable physiological and physical conditions, those mental objects that hold our attention determine our action. Because our propensities naturally hold our attention, it takes no effort to act in accordance with them. Similarly, it takes little effort to act in accordance with a well-established habit. The only way that the weaker, more abstract and ideal objects motivate our actions, according to James, is through artificial reinforcement. This artificial reinforcement is the mental effort of voluntary attention. Without this volitional effort, James argues, there can be no morality. Thus, for James, the exertion of a certain kind of mental effort is the essence of moral action. In his own words, *"To sustain a representation, to think,* is, in short, the only moral act . . ." (PP, 1170, italics James's; see also TT, 109–10).

According to James, acting in accordance with our propensities and habits is acting in the line of less resistance, whereas acting morally is acting in the line of greater resistance. Because certain states of mind tend to call up similar states, James notes that there is great resistance to the attempt to concentrate on a thought that is out of step with the others that fill our mind at the moment. But if we insist on concentrating on the quieter voice, it will begin to call up associations of its own. Continued concentration eventually fills the mind with associations of this new thought, and the thoughts that had originally been stronger are driven out. When the new thoughts prevail in our mind, they lead to their own, different actions in accordance with the process of ideomotor action.

The key to the triumph of these new thoughts, James observes, is often a function of naming a thing correctly. If an alcoholic is tempted to take a drink, his success in overcoming his temptation will probably be in direct relation to his resistance to the propensity to rationalize the action away as something other than the manifestation of the alcoholism it truly is.

It is important to note a significant consequence of James's understanding of the will. As James describes it, the will is a selective and not a creative faculty.[13] The essence of the will, for James, is nothing other than the ability to keep a thought in the mind that, if left to itself, would be crowded out. This implies that the will, like voluntary movements, is secondary. We have already seen that James holds voluntary movements to be secondary, as they involve a selection from movements initially presented to consciousness through primary instinctual or emotional movements. Similarly, James holds that the will itself is a secondary faculty. It is powerless to put new ideas into the mind. Instead, it must wait for these ideas to be placed in the mind through perception. The function of the will is merely to choose from the given possibilities the one that seems most likely to achieve the desired ends.

There is a close connection between James's view of social change and his psychology at this point. We saw in the last chapter that James believes social evolution to be dependent on the presentation of creative ideas by geniuses and on their selection by non-geniuses. We also saw that James holds the origin of geniuses to be in a cycle of operation different from that of the community of non-geniuses that does the selecting. In a similar way, in James's psychology, thoughts originate in a cycle of operation different from the one responsible for their selection. Since the will is the faculty of selection, it follows that whatever novelty there is in the world is, strictly speaking, not a product of the human will.

Given that the proper role of the Jamesian will is one of selection and not of creation, is its execution of this role free or determined? If our wills are free, we have the capacity to vary the duration and intensity of our effort of attention. If our wills are not free, the amount of effort we exert is determined. Although we certainly *feel* as though we are free to determine our own level of exertion, James admits that this is not sufficient to prove that our wills *are* free. He points out, for example, that this feeling of freedom attends our effortless volitions but that, in these cases, our volition is not free (PP, 1175–6).

James argues that the question of whether our wills are free or not cannot be answered on strictly psychological grounds. It is impossible to determine whether we *might* have exerted more or less effort than we actually did exert. James claims that psychology does not need to answer this question in order to carry out its scientific investigations. Psychology, he argues, deals only with the general laws of volition. It begins with the effort applied and does not need to question its cause.[14]

Although James argues that the question of the freedom of the will is not a psychological question, he contends that there are practical grounds for deciding the question. He observes that most psychologists deny the freedom of the will, in practice, because their task of science-building calls for the elimination of independent variables from the equations. In opposition to this, James believes there are important moral and religious reasons for believing in free will. Without freedom in the exertion of the effort of volition, life, for James, seems meaningless. He suggests, in fact, that this exertion may be the one "strictly underived and original contribution which we make to the world" (PP, 1182).

I want to make one final point before leaving James's discussion of the will, and with that, of his psychology. It may be helpful to understand James's view of the will more fully if we apply it to Kant's discussion of morality. Although this is an unusual application, it can be of help both for understanding the Jamesian will and for understanding Kant's views on the relation between inclination and duty in moral actions.

According to Kant, duty dictates the correct answer to every moral decision. But, he argues, moral agents are not coerced into following their duty, and if they do follow their duty, they may do so for the wrong motivation. Thus, Kant identifies three possible relations between duty and action. First, it may be that an action is not in accordance with duty. In this case, the action is evil and must be condemned. Second, an action may be in *accordance* with duty but not *from* duty; that is, it may be the action duty calls for yet be motivated by inclination and not by duty. In this case, an action may be useful and honorable, but it cannot be esteemed as a moral action. Third, an action may be both in *accordance* with duty and *from* duty; that is, it may be the action duty calls for and be motivated by duty. For Kant, it is only in this last case that an action is a moral one.[15]

This view has caused some embarrassment for Kant's followers because it leads to some rather strange conclusions about morality. For example, because moral actions are actions not in accordance with our inclinations, it seems that we can never take pleasure in acting morally. Furthermore, the more evil a person's inclinations are—the greater the difference between what he wants to do and what he should do— the greater his capacity for morality. Conversely, it seems that a person who always wants to do what she should cannot be moral at all.

These seem to be strange conclusions indeed until we realize that Kant does not apply the term "moral" to all praiseworthy actions, but only to certain kinds of actions—namely, to those motivated by duty. He claims, for example, that actions in accordance with duty but not from duty may not only be useful and honorable, but may even deserve praise and encouragement. Because Kant does not stress this difference between praiseworthy and moral actions, however, many commentators try to soften his statements and claim that he does not really mean what he says. Strangely enough, James seems to agree with Kant that not all praiseworthy actions are moral and that moral action is different from action in accordance with inclination. By applying James's psychology of moral action to Kant's theory, we can explain the latter in such a way that further reduces the strangeness of the conclusions to which it leads.[16]

As previously discussed, the essence of morality for James is volitional effort. It is the means by which we make the weaker impulse in our consciousness the stronger. Without it, the strength of our inclinations would overwhelm the still, small voice that recommends the moral course of action. If we act in accordance with our strong inclinations, it may be—depending on the nature of these inclinations— that we effect good, but we are not acting morally. If, on the other hand, we lend the effort of attention to the weaker impulse so constantly that it begins to wax stronger and to call up other allies until the inclinations are driven out of the mind, then our actions will be moral ones. Thus, for James, morality always involves the overthrow of stronger impulses by means of effort.[17] Where there is no effort, there can be no morality.

Applying this to Kant's theory, we see that it is reasonable to link motivation and morality. If an action is motivated by inclination, it requires no effort to will it, and is thus not moral. If an action is motivated by duty, which is naturally a weaker motivator than inclination, its performance always requires effort and is thus moral.

This brings us to the end of our examination of James's views of the psychological makeup of the finite, individual self. This examination has clarified the nature of the individual that is at the center of James's individualism. We have seen that James understands the individual self in terms of the reflex action model, a model that involves a teleological relation among the functions of perception, conception, and volition. We have also noted tensions in the Jamesian individual. These tensions involve the conflicting needs of the individual both to remain true to the flux of experience and to make useful selections from that flux. Despite James's frequent references to reflex action theory, its centrality for James's psychology and philosophy has largely been overlooked by commentators. In chapter 4, we will see how this oversight often leads to interpretations of James that do violence to his thought by, in effect, snipping the reflex arc.

In the next chapter, which focuses on the metaphysical dimensions of the self, we will explore both the Jamesian self and its tensions in still greater detail. We will see that, while a social discussion of the self takes us outside of the individual self, a metaphysical analysis leads us even deeper into the self than we are able to go with the help of psychology. This deeper look is also dangerous, however, because it brings to light severe tensions that are not at all easy to resolve.

CHAPTER 3

Eternal Dimensions of
James's Individualism

In this chapter, we turn to James's discussion of the individual self in its relation to the larger spiritual world of which he believes it to be a part. This examination of the individualism in James's metaphysics will yield not only more complexity and richness but also more tension than is to be found in the individualism of his social philosophy or in that of his psychology. The tension is so great, in fact, that it can cause real problems in understanding James's position. At some points, especially in his discussion of religion, it seems doubtful whether James's individualism extends to his metaphysics at all. Working through this doubt, we will find that James is, indeed, an individualist on this level. In fact, the individualism of his metaphysics is more radical than that of either his social philosophy or his psychology. This is a point we will emphasize at the end of chapter 5 by comparing James's individualism to that of other nineteenth-century individualists.

It is not enough, however, simply to determine *that* James's individualism extends to his metaphysics. We must also determine what *kind* of metaphysical individualism James adopts. In doing so, we will come face to face with the diachronic dynamism in James's individualism. We have already explored the volitional individualism that seems to prevail in James's sociological and psychological discussions. Now we will see that he apparently presents a very different kind of individualism in *Varieties of Religious Experience*. Here, James's emphasis on perception more than on volition results in a perceptual individualism. It can seem, at times, that the volitional individualism James

59

has presented earlier has nothing to do with this later perceptual individualism. In Part II, we will take up the task of reconciling these two individualisms, showing how James moves toward their integration in the last few years of his life. The task of this present chapter is merely to work out the individualism in James's metaphysics. We must examine it as thoroughly as possible without trying, as yet, to resolve the tensions this examination will reveal.

James's writings on the metaphysical self are located principally in the texts from two series of lectures he delivered in Britain. The first series, the Gifford Lectures delivered in 1901 and 1902, was published under the title *The Varieties of Religious Experience*. James's purpose in this work is to conduct a psychological investigation into the nature and value of the religious experience to which the individual self is susceptible. Because James's investigation focuses on individual religious experience (on what he calls "personal religion"), it provides a new level of complexity for his understanding of the self. And because his investigation is grounded in the psychological view of the self, our work in the last chapter is indispensable for understanding James's views in this chapter.

The more complex self, as developed in *Varieties*, puts pressure on the terms of the reflex action model of the self we examined in such detail in the last chapter. Although all three faculties of reflex action are present here in some form, *Varieties* places undue emphasis on perception. The reflex arc degenerates badly because of the attenuation of the roles of conception and volition. Although the attenuation is partly due to the fact that James focuses, not on religious *thought* or on religious *action*, but on religious *experience*, not all of the attenuation can be explained in this way. (It would certainly be possible to emphasize the perception involved in religious experience without taking away from the roles of conception and volition.) The attenuation of these two faculties of the reflex arc is also due to two biases with which James approaches his study of religious experience. In the first part of this chapter, I will take up these biases in detail and examine closely the complexity and tension to be found in this first series of lectures.

The second series of lectures, the Hibbert Lectures delivered at Oxford in 1908 and 1909, was subsequently published as *A Pluralistic Universe*. James's goal in these lectures is to defend his own metaphysical view, radical empiricism, against its rivals, theism and idealism. In the second part of this chapter, I will present James's defense of radical empiricism, a defense made possible by a self-confessed change of mind on James's part. In chapter 5, I will show how crucial this change of mind is for James's mature individualism.

WJ's 2 biases

THE VARIETIES OF RELIGIOUS EXPERIENCE ① *anti-institutionalism*

② anti-intellectualism elitism genuises

Even a cursory reading of *Varieties* bears out my earlier claim that this work is grounded in James's psychology. Since James himself indicates that his study is psychological in nature (VRE, 12), it is not surprising that it presupposes the reflex action model of the self. For James, the psychological self is at work in religion. Consequently, the faculties of perception, conception, and volition are present and related in a teleological way. Furthermore, for James, elements of religious experience are intrinsically no different from those of other types of experience. They differ only in object. Religious sentiments are normal sentiments aimed at religious objects (VRE, 31). The essential function of the religious self is to experience the world and then to act on it. Thinking serves as an intermediary step between experience and action that can provide useful direction in achieving desired goals.

With this connection established between *Varieties* and James's psychology, it is also important to point out that James's application of the reflex action model of the self to religion is not without its problems. Although James's work in *Varieties* is of great value and full of rich insight, tensions develop in it because of two biases with which he approaches his study. In chapter 1, I noted James's anti-institutionalism in religion. Closely related to this is a strong anti-intellectual bias in his understanding of religion. This anti-intellectualism is expressed in *Varieties* in the view that conception is a secondary and even inessential faculty for religion. This leaves perception and volition as the primary faculties of the religious self. James's second bias tends toward the dislocation of volition, resulting in a work that overemphasizes the role of perception. This second bias, which I will call the elitism of *Varieties*, is expressed in James's decision to concern himself principally with the extreme cases of religious experience, with the experiences of what he terms religious geniuses. Because of the particular relation between genius and volition, this bias results in a work that displaces volition in a way that is hard to reconcile with the more balanced presentation of the reflex action model in *Principles* and that is especially hard to reconcile with the volitional religion of the *Will to Believe*. Great as these tensions are, there is also indication in *Varieties* itself that James's thought is beginning the development that will eventually make their resolution possible. It will be the central thesis of chapter 5 that James underwent a gradual conversion in his thinking in the last ten years of his life, and it will be my task in that chapter to try to minimize the tensions in *Varieties* by suggesting a way to rethink it in light of this conversion. But in order to appreciate fully the importance of James's conversion, we must see more clearly the precise nature of the tensions in *Varieties*. This requires a detailed look at the two biases I have identified.

The Subordination of Reason

James's first bias, his anti-intellectual approach to religion, is already hinted at in the title of the book. James's decision to look for instruction in religion to the various types of religious *experience* that have been recorded by religious geniuses and to have little to do with the theological contributions that the intellect has made to the subject is an indication of what is to come. For James, religion and the religious self are principally functions of experience and not of theory.

James's position in *Varieties* is not only that the intellect is secondary for religion, but also that it is inessential to it. He writes:

> The theories which Religion generates, being thus variable, are secondary; and if you wish to grasp her essence, you must look to the feelings and the conduct as being the more constant elements. It is between these two elements that the short circuit exists on which she carries on her principal business, while the ideas and symbols and other institutions form loop-lines which may be perfections and improvements, and may even some day all be united into one harmonious system, but which are not to be regarded as organs with an indispensable function, necessary at all times for religious life to go on. (VRE, 397)

James's point here is that perception and volition are the only faculties essential to religion and that they could perform religious functions without the aid of the intellect.

James does not, however, leave the intellect out of the picture entirely. There is a certain irony in the fact that, much as James emphasizes experience in *Varieties*, his treatment of it is intellectual. While James quotes many firsthand accounts of religious experience and the conduct to which it leads, his method of examining these accounts is intellectual. In fact, James's statement that his study is a psychological one indicates that his examination is intended to be scientific.

Given this irony, what is the value of the intellect for religion? The intellect, James argues, is powerless to contribute to the experience that is religion's principal concern. Nor is the intellect capable of giving this experience an indubitable epistemological foundation. As we saw in our discussion of James's social individualism in chapter 1, James contends that the best the intellect can do is to take on the critical role of comparing various religious beliefs. He writes that, if philosophy will "abandon metaphysics and deduction for criticism and induction, and frankly transform herself from theology into science of religions, she can make herself enormously useful" (VRE, 359). Through the science of religions, the intellect could work to divest religion of the local and accidental accretions to which it is susceptible, in order to reduce inessential differences between various religionists. The intellect could also work to keep religion from compromising itself by contradicting new scientific findings. The resulting religious hypotheses would not be *provable* by the intellect, but the intellect could ensure that they are *possible*, thus leaving the way open for individual belief. With this understanding of the science of religions, it is clear that James intends *Varieties* to be a contribution toward its founding.

Helpful as the intellect can be when used in this legitimate way, James is quite wary of its power. Because this power is so often used improperly, James warns that the intellect poses a threat to the other two faculties. Because the intellect is verbal, it is able to formulate arguments that threaten to overwhelm the less loquacious parts of the self. James writes:

> Philosophy lives in words, but truth and fact well up into our lives in ways that exceed verbal formulation. There is in the living act of perception always something that glimmers and twinkles and will not be caught, and for which reflection comes too late. No one knows this as well as the philosopher. He must fire his volley of new vocables out of his conceptual shotgun, for his profession condemns him to this industry, but he secretly knows the hollowness and irrelevancy. . . . In the religious sphere, in particular, belief that formulas are true can never wholly take the place of personal experience. (VRE, 360)

Philosophers, however, tend to forget the ultimate "hollowness and irrelevancy" of their verbal constructions, and in the religious sphere, formulaic beliefs in the form of powerful orthodoxies tend to eclipse, or at least to repress, personal experience.

James's strong words against the intellect are in keeping with his general anti-intellectual position in *Varieties*. James distinguishes between perception and reflection and leaves no doubt as to which he considers more important. Because reflection always "comes too late" to catch the truths of perception, he sees an ultimate "hollowness and irrelevancy" in conceptualization. In religion, this means James is on the side of

W J for

personal, experiential religion in opposition to public, confessional religion. As we will see in the next chapters, however, this is not James's final word on this topic. He eventually works to overcome the tension between perception and conception that is so prevalent in *Varieties*.

The fear of intellectual tyranny James expresses in *Varieties* points to the connection between his sociological and his psychological views. For James, there is a link between the public and institutional in the social realm and the intellectual in the psychological realm. This link is clear in the passage I quoted at the beginning of this section, in which he identifies "ideas and symbols and other institutions" as intellectual tools. In our discussion of the social self in chapter 1, we noted James's religious anti-institutionalism. One consequence of James's linking institutions with the intellect is the close relation of his anti-institutionalism with his anti-intellectualism. Both James's anti-institutionalism and his anti-intellectualism are functions of the individualism James espouses in *Varieties*. At this point in his thinking, James's individualism expresses itself in social terms as the defense of the individual against institutional tyranny and in psychological terms as the defense of the individualizing faculties against the tyranny of the intellect.

The combativeness of James's individualism here shows not only that James is on the defensive against social institutions, but also that he is internally divided against himself. He recognizes that the intellect has great value and power, but distrusts the use to which that power might be put. As I have already indicated, this is not the point at which James leaves his individualism. In Part II, I will show that James eventually modifies his views about the intellect and that he works toward its integration with the other faculties. In *Varieties*, however, James's individualism is firmly entrenched in anti-institutionalism and anti-intellectualism.

With these connections in mind, it is only to be expected that a text as strongly anti-intellectual as *Varieties* would also emphasize a defense of the individual over against the institution. That is, in fact, precisely the case. From the beginning, James makes it clear not only that his interest is with the personal religious experience of the individual, but also that this personal experience is quintessential religion. James argues that churches are founded by individuals whose religious experience occurs directly between them and the divine and is not mediated by institutions. The churches these individuals subsequently found, says James, "live at second-hand upon tradition," and their members lead a "second-hand religious life" composed of a "mass of suggested feeling and imitated conduct" (VRE, 15, 32–4). At the end of *Varieties*, James makes one of the strongest cases for individualism he makes anywhere. He writes:

> I think . . . that however particular questions connected with our individual destinies may be answered, it is only by acknowledging them as genuine questions, and living in the sphere of thought which they open up, that we become profound. But to live thus is to be religious. . . . By being religious we establish ourselves in possession of ultimate reality at the only points at which reality is given us to guard. Our responsible concern is with our private destiny, after all. (VRE, 394–5)

James then goes on to explain that the reason for his individualism is the same as the reason for his emphasis on feeling and subordination of intellect in religion. That reason is that "Individuality is founded in feeling." Furthermore, James contends, it is through our feelings that we have the most direct access to reality (VRE, 395).

The tension in the reflex action model at this point is palpable. For James, the power of the intellect, seen in the light of its essential deficiency, renders it very dangerous. That is, the ability of the intellect to speak and the compelling nature of its logical formulations give it a power the other two faculties do not have. Yet, James argues, the words and logical formulations of the intellect are inherently incapable of an exhaustive representation of reality. This amounts to a resurfacing of the tension we noted in *Principles* between several of the basic characteristics of the stream of consciousness. For James, consciousness is in continuous, constant flux, but it is also selective, treating different parts of the flux differently. Conscious selves thus have a loyalty divided between the flux of experience and the stability of useful selections from this flux. In *Varieties*, this divided loyalty results in severe tension. James seems to be playing favorites here, emphasizing the flux at the expense of selection. That is, he protects perception from conception. But this protection is complicated by his ambivalent stance toward conception. Because of the power of the intellect, James considers it to be, potentially, a dangerous enemy. Yet it is not for this reason to be exiled, since it has important, albeit secondary, contributions to make to the self. The result is an unsustainable dialectical tension, where the tendency is to push the intellect out of its place in reflex action because of its dangerous power and, at the same time, to welcome it because of its helpful contributions. This explains the ultimately suspicious, grudging, and defensive acceptance of the intellect in *Varieties*.

Severe as this tension is, it is not the only one to be found in *Varieties*. James's justification for his anti-intellectualism also raises the question of the value of volition. If perception both founds our individuality and gives us our access to reality, it is unclear that volition has any but a secondary role to play. This second tension, which we will explore in detail in the next section, further endangers the balance of the reflex action model of the self and threatens the consistency of *Varieties* with James's earlier works.

Perception and Volition

The subordination of reason raises the question of the relation of the remaining faculties of perception and volition. Is perception or is volition the more central faculty of the Jamesian self? James's move toward integration in the last years of his life eventually takes him beyond this question. But at this stage in his thinking, it is a question of some importance. Strong arguments could be made for the priority both of perception and of volition. In *Principles*, as well as in the *Will to Believe*, James seems to argue quite clearly for the priority of volition. In "Reflex Action and Theism," James's teleological conception of the self entails that the will is the most important of the human faculties. James there writes, "The willing department of our nature . . . dominates both the conceiving department and the feeling department; or, in plainer English, perception and thinking are only there for behavior's sake" (WB, 92). In *Principles*, James argues that our very perception is guided by our interest; that our feelings are determined, in part, by our volition. In his essay "The Will to Believe," James argues that the will must decide genuine options in social, moral, and religious areas. It is in these areas that faith in a fact often helps to create the fact. In these works, James seems to be arguing, in almost existentialist fashion, that the will is the individuating faculty of the self. Nevertheless, in opposition to all these arguments, we have just seen that, in *Varieties*, James claims that individuality is founded in feeling and that it is through feeling that we come the closest to reality. What are we to make of this at least apparent inconsistency?

I believe one reason *Varieties* seems so far out of step with James's earlier writings is because of the second bias I referred to earlier—namely, elitism. We have already noted that James focuses on the experience of religious geniuses in *Varieties*. He does so on the assumption that these extreme cases give the clearest picture of the essential characteristics of religious experience. He writes that the essential quality of religious experiences is "most prominent and easy to notice in those religious experiences which are most one-sided, exaggerated, and intense" (VRE, 44). Application to the religious experience of non-geniuses is then possible by extrapolation from the experience of geniuses. This approach presupposes that religious experiences of varying degrees of intensity are on a continuum; that is, that the religious experiences of geniuses are like those of non-geniuses, only more so. James implicitly assumes that there is no point that radically separates the religious experiences of geniuses from those of non-geniuses. But this assumption is problematic.

James's account of geniuses in *Principles* shows a way in which the general experience of geniuses differs from that of non-geniuses. In chapter 2, we noted James's claim that geniuses are guided so well by their involuntary attention that they often do not need to develop their ability to control their attention voluntarily. This means that volition need not play a large role in the discussion of the experiences of geniuses, although volition is crucial for understanding the experiences of non-geniuses.

Unfortunately, it seems that James does not take this distinction into account in his discussion of religious experience in *Varieties*. Starting from the viewpoint of religious geniuses, James emphasizes experience at the expense of the volitional role of faith. The type of religious experience James emphasizes in *Varieties* is one in which the practical results of an experience are applied automatically, obviating the need for the volitional appropriation of the experience. Although I will reserve the term religious genius for those who do not need the will *after* religious experience, it is important to point out that James subordinates the role of the will *before* and *during* religious experience, as well. In his discussion of conversion, James takes up the role of volition prior to religious experience. He distinguishes between a volitional type of conversion and a self-surrender type. He hardly does more than mention the first type, in which the will plays a role in conversion, but emphasizes the second type, where conversion seems to take place on the subconscious level, independently of the will. James writes:

> Of the volitional type of conversion it would be easy to give examples, but they are as a rule less interesting than those of the self-surrender type, in which the subconscious effects are more abundant and often startling. I will therefore hurry to the latter, the more so because the difference between the two types is after all not radical. Even in the most voluntarily built-up sort of regeneration there are passages of partial self-surrender interposed; and in the great majority of all cases, when the will has done its uttermost towards

bringing one close to the complete unification aspired after, it seems that the very last step must be left to other forces and performed without the help of its activity. In other words, self-surrender becomes then indispensable. (VRE, 170–1)

In keeping with his subordination of the will before and after religious experience, James does not discuss any role it might play during religious experience.

I will have much more to say in chapter 6 about the role of the will before, during, and after special experiences. The point I want to stress here is that James takes as the fundamental type the experience of religious geniuses, for whom volition is displaced in the aftermath of religious experience. Most of us, however, are not religious geniuses, and religious perception requires from us a volitional response. Unfortunately, James fails to introduce volition as an ingredient of the religious experience of non-geniuses, an ingredient whose function cannot be extrapolated from the experience of geniuses. This failure severely limits the applicability of James's analysis to the religious experience of ordinary persons and constitutes the elitism of *Varieties*.

At this point, it should be clear how the details support my earlier claims about the tensions in *Varieties*. We can now see how James's anti-intellectualism and his elitism in this work contribute to the attenuation of two of the faculties of reflex action. It seems clear that, in *Varieties*, conception and volition are second in rank to perception. I have also emphasized, however, that attenuation is not elimination. In the case of conception, I have pointed out its role in the establishment of the science of religions. I have yet to point out the attenuated role of volition in *Varieties*. I will turn to this task now by means of a discussion of Julius Bixler's interpretation of the roles of perception and volition in *Varieties* and in James's thought in general. It will be my contention that, although Bixler presents many helpful insights into James's work, the simplicity of his interpretation does not allow him to account for the complex, albeit attenuated, role of volition in *Varieties*. My discussion of Bixler will naturally lead into a detailed examination of James's analysis of religious experience. This, in turn, will bring to light more of the complexity of James's religious discussion of the individual.

Bixler's Bifurcation

Bixler does not approach the tension between perception and volition in *Varieties* from the standpoint of James's psychology, as we are doing, so he does not couch the problem in these terms. He speaks, instead, of what he calls a "contrast between two philosophies of life."[1] Bixler claims that this contrast can be seen most clearly in the introduction to *The Literary Remains of the Late Henry James*, where William James introduces a posthumously published volume of his father's work. In his introduction to this volume, James distinguishes, as we noted in chapter 1, between moralism and religion, where moralism is the pluralistic view we tend toward when feeling strong and healthy, and religion is the monistic view we tend toward when feeling weak and vulnerable. Bixler traces this bifurcation through various aspects of James's work, including his biography, his epistemology, his psychology, and his philosophy of religion. In discussing the last point, Bixler takes up *Varieties*, in which James makes a distinction between what he calls healthy-minded and morbid-minded religion. Bixler identifies this distinction in *Varieties* with James's earlier distinction between moralistic pluralism and religious monism. Bixler associates both moralistic pluralism and healthy-minded religion with action, with "put[ting] on the whole armor of God," and he associates both religious monism and morbid-minded religion with contemplation, with "rest[ing] on the everlasting arms."[2]

Bixler's bifurcation is simple and, to a degree, helpful for understanding some of the conflict in James's life and work. Unfortunately, it is too simple to be true to the complexity in James's thought. This is due largely to the fact that it takes its bearings from James's dualistic introduction to *Literary Remains*, in which he clearly contrasts active moralism and passive religion. Bixler's interpretation fails to take sufficient account of either the psychological grounding of *Varieties* or the development in James's thought during the fifteen years between his writing of the introduction to *Literary Remains* and his drafting of *Varieties*. Because it does not take sufficient account of the psychological grounding of *Varieties*, Bixler's interpretation is incapable of dealing with certain complexities in James's views. For example, it cannot deal with the tensions surrounding the proper role of the intellect in the reflex action model. This deficiency is particularly serious in light of the fact that James's later work concentrates so heavily on the resolution of these tensions. Because it does not take sufficient account of the development of James's thought, Bixler's interpretation leads to a rather severe distortion of *Varieties* in trying to make it fit the dualistic structure of the introduction to *Literary Remains*.

By trying to force the bifurcation of the introduction to *Literary Remains* onto *Varieties*, Bixler misses the fact that James makes two different distinctions in *Varieties*. The first distinction is between moralism and religion. Moralism, for James, involves at best a stoic acceptance of the universe, whereas religion embraces the universe wholeheartedly (VRE, 41–50, esp. 44–6). The second distinction is between two types of religion, which I will call R_1 and R_2. R_1 is "healthy-minded religion," and R_2 is the religion of the "morbid-minded" (VRE, 71–138, esp. 109ff). To label moralism, R_1, or R_2 either as exclusively active or as exclusively contemplative is inaccurate. James refers, in various places in *Varieties*, to each as active and to each as contemplative.[3] Bixler's bifurcation leaves us without recourse in resolving this apparent inconsistency. Approaching this question from the standpoint of the psychology of the individual, on the other hand, allows us to do justice to the complexity of *Varieties*, noting in what respect James considers each of these worldviews to be active and in what respect contemplative.

According to Bixler's interpretation, each worldview James considers grounds itself exclusively in one faculty. The differences between worldviews arise because of their commitment to different faculties. Thus, moralism and R_1 ground themselves in volition, whereas R_2 grounds itself in perception.[4] But we have seen that, despite the tensions placed on the reflex action model of the self, it is still intact in *Varieties*. This means that this model underlies each of these worldviews. Thus, moralism, R_1, and R_2 each involve perception, conception, and volition. The differences among these views arise, not from the exclusive acceptance of different faculties, but from the variations of emphasis each places on the several faculties of reflex action.[5]

There is one more point to be made before we examine in detail the different ways moralism, R_1, and R_2 emphasize the faculties of reflex action. I have been careful to point out that James's discussion of religion is grounded in his psychology. It is just as important to note that, for James, religion goes beyond psychology. An understanding of the internal relations of the individual psyche is crucial for understanding James's views on religion, but religion goes beyond these internal relations to the eternal relations between the self and God.

So far in this chapter, the discussion has centered largely around the role of various parts of the self in religious experience. We are now ready to move to a more direct discussion of religion. In *Varieties*, James concentrates on the human side of the human–divine nexus that results in religious experience. Only at the end of the book does he allow himself to sketch out briefly what he calls his "over-beliefs" about the divine side of that nexus. In *A Pluralistic Universe*, James lays out his over-beliefs in greater detail. The ways in which the metaphysical self is more complex than the psychological self will become clearer as we work through James's discussions in these two texts. We will focus on the various manifestations of religious experience, on the way the subconscious mediates between the human and the divine in conversion, on the nature of the divine self, and on the relation between the human self and the divine self.

The Definition of Religion

In seeking to define religion in *Varieties*, James realizes the impossibility of identifying its absolute essence. In *Principles*, as we saw in chapter 2, James holds essences to be not absolute, but context-dependent. In *Varieties*, James contends that mistaking an abstract, context-dependent essence for the thing itself is an example of the fundamental mistake of "absolutism and one-sided dogmatism." The impossibility of identifying the absolute essence of religion is further shown by the widespread disagreement among those who claim to have arrived at such an essence. James concludes that "the word 'religion' cannot stand for any single principle or essence, but is rather a collective name" (VRE, 30). In order to identify his topic for the lectures, James does define religion, but he is careful to point out that his definition is not exhaustive. It is the identification of the essence of religion as determined by the context of a particular investigation.

For the purposes of his lectures, James defines religion as "the feelings, acts, and experiences of individual men in their solitude, so far as they apprehend themselves to stand in relation to whatever they may consider the divine" (VRE, 34, italics deleted). In defining religion as feelings, acts, and experiences, James emphasizes the faculty of perception and the conduct to which it leads. The intellectual faculty, although not as important, is not without a role to play, since "it is evident that out of religion in the sense in which we take it, theologies, philosophies, and ecclesiastical organizations may secondarily grow" (VRE, 34). The sociological way of putting this same point is that, since religion proper belongs to individual persons in their solitude, the institutional religion of church and theology—which, as we noted in chapter 1, James holds to be a social product of the intellect—is relegated to second rank.

James points out that the divine in his definition must be taken neither too narrowly nor too broadly. It would be too narrow, he contends, to require it to be a concrete deity. This would exclude Emersonianism and Buddhism from being religions. To keep this from happening, any object that is god*like* must be acceptable as divine. But it would be too broad, James argues, to accept the divine as merely whatever is "most primal and enveloping and real." Instead, James takes the divine to mean "only such a primal reality as the individual feels impelled to respond to solemnly and gravely, and neither by a curse nor a jest" (VRE, 39).

James's distinction between moralism and religion can be succinctly described as referring to two different ways individuals can accept the universe. James argues that, although both moralists and religionists have a finite place in the order of things, they respond to their finitude in different ways. Moralists accept it only because they must. Their muscles are tensed in struggle against the order of things. Religionists, on the other hand, accept, welcome, and even love the universe and their finite place in it. Moralists respond willfully; religionists, passionately. Paradoxically, however, the result of these responses is that moralists are on the defensive and find it harder to act in the world, whereas religionists are free to be aggressive in their active relations with the world.

There is an old story of a man who was traveling a long road with a heavy pack on his back. A kindly farmer drew up beside him in his wagon and offered him a ride. The traveler gladly accepted. He climbed up on the wagon and, still wearing his pack, gratefully sat down beside the farmer. After riding in silence for a few minutes, the farmer asked the traveler why he was still wearing his pack. "You will be much more comfortable if you throw your pack into the back of the wagon," he said. "Oh," said the traveler, "it is so kind of you to give me a ride. I wouldn't want you to have to carry my pack, as well." For James, the moralist is like this traveler. He does not have the strength to travel the road under his own power. But he surrenders only what he must, and, teeth gritted, continues to carry what he can. The religionist, on the other hand, gladly clambers aboard the wagon and tosses his pack into the back. He embraces the surrender required by his finitude and gives up all struggle against it in order to maximize his joy. In helping to make this necessary surrender easier for us, James argues, religion shows itself to be "an essential organ of our life, performing a function which no other portion of our nature can so successfully fulfill" (VRE, 49).[6]

James's distinction between R_1 and R_2 describes a difference in the way individuals can respond to evil. Healthy-minded persons respond willfully, warring against the very presence of evil, while morbid-minded persons respond passively, allying themselves with a higher power that does not eradicate evil, but that promises victory over it. In light of the initial surrender involved in R_1, which James describes as in no essential experiential way different from the Lutheran

involuntary healthy minded
innocent, only see good
W/ Whit men

or Wesleyan conversion of R_2, it would be a mistake to describe it as merely active. On the other hand, because of its active fight against evil, it would be a mistake to describe it as merely passive or contemplative. It is clear that R_1 shares characteristics of both the moralism and the religion described in the introduction to *Literary Remains* as being strongly disjunctive. There James writes, "The accord of moralism and religion is superficial, their discord radical. Only the deepest thinkers on both sides see that one must go" (ERM, 63). Now, in *Varieties*, it seems that R_1 is James's attempt to bridge this radical discord by working to reconcile what he had earlier thought irreconcilable. This is the indication I alluded to earlier that James's thoughts are beginning to move in the direction of integration. As we will see in the next chapter, this change gathers momentum in James's thought and finally amounts to a conversion that overcomes much of the tension I have pointed out thus far.

Healthy-Minded Religion (R_1)

James's discussion of this first type of religion, under the heading of "The Religion of Healthy-Mindedness," can be misleading if we expect too much uniformity. One consequence of defining religion to be primarily a personal matter is that there then exist as many different religions as there are persons with religious experience. James's discussion of R_1 might just as accurately have been titled "The Religions of Healthy-Mindedness." Of course, similarities in this experience lead to similarities in the religions. For this reason, it is not wrong to speak of a type of religion, as long as we keep in mind that the category is somewhat arbitrary and that it stands for a range of similar, but not identical, religious views. Although I will continue to refer to R_1 in the singular, as James did, it is important not to lose sight of this plurality.

According to James, R_1 can be either voluntary or involuntary. In its latter form, it occurs naturally in innocent souls who seem simply incapable of seeing anything other than the rosy side of life. Their "sunshiny" disposition is an immediate response to the world. Those who practice voluntary religious optimism, on the other hand, see at least some of the evil in the universe, but deliberately choose to ignore or deny it. Their voluntary optimism constitutes a systematic, abstract way of conceiving that allows them to select the goodness of a thing as its essence and to ignore its other aspects. James cites Whitman as an example of someone who selects "good as the essential and universal aspect of being" and ignores its evil aspects (VRE, 75ff), and he gives two examples of religious movements based on *involuntary religion — nature (evolution)*

mind cure movement

voluntary healthy-mindedness. The first, which James touches on briefly, is the religion of nature, so strongly influenced by natural science and, in particular, by the theory of evolution. The second, which James describes in detail and to which I now turn, is the "mind-cure movement."

James describes the mind-cure movement as a collection of similar religious strains influenced by the Gospels, New England transcendentalism, Berkeleyan idealism, spiritism, evolutionism in its popular, optimistic form, and Hinduism. He identifies optimism as the most characteristic feature of the movement and as that which binds together these widely varying influences. Adherents to this movement are convinced that great good can be done by thinking positively about the world and by forgetting its negative aspects.

Although positive thinking does not cure all evils or work equally well for everyone, James points out that its results are often significant and long-lasting. Through the power of suggestion and a great use of the subconscious, the mind-cure movement is responsible for the cure of many chronic physical ailments and for the moral and emotional enrichment of many of its practitioners.

The mind-cure movement, James continues, holds to the presupposition that he believes forms the basis of all religious experience. This presupposition is that human beings have a dual nature—a shallower and a deeper side—and that we can choose which side we want to live out of. The deeper side is that of religion, whereas the shallower side is "that of the fleshly sensations, instincts, and desires, of egotism, doubt, and the lower personal interests" (VRE, 86). What separates the mind-cure movement from other conceptions of religious experience is its identification of the cause of the difficulty of leaving this shallower side behind. Christianity, for example, claims the cause is "frowardness." Mind-cure claims it is fear.

For some, positive thinking seems to be the natural way of viewing the world. Others find it more difficult to leave the shallower self behind to identify with the larger, optimistic self. In these cases, a religionist might go through a process of conversion to pass from one stage of existence to the other. We will turn in some detail to the topic of conversion after taking a closer look at James's understanding of R₂.

Before we turn to R_2, however, I should point out that my description of R_1 is really an interpretation. Although this interpretation minimizes inconsistencies in James's account, it does not eliminate all of them. The remaining areas of inconsistency in his description of R_1, three of which I will now point out, make an interpretation necessary and suggest that his thought, beginning with the duality of *Literary Remains* and moving to the more complex understanding in *Varieties*, is still under development.

Varieties of Religion experience was still developing his theories — more complex explanation fewer inconsistencies in later works [handwritten annotation]

The first area of inconsistency in James's account involves the relation between moralism and R_1. Once or twice, James himself blurs the distinction between moralism and R_1 that he makes at the beginning of *Varieties*, slipping back into the dualistic contrast between moralism and religion of the introduction to *Literary Remains*. At one point, he describes the opposing views of the Methodist convert and the "healthy-minded moralist" (VRE, 140). At another point, James writes that Stoicism and Epicureanism "mark the conclusion of what we call the once-born period, and represent the highest flights of what twice-born religion would call the purely natural man" (VRE, 121–2). Since James has earlier identified Stoicism with moralism (VRE, 41–50), it seems he is now linking moralism with once-born religion; hence, with healthy-mindedness. This is, of course, not the way James usually expresses himself in *Varieties*. He spends a lot of time setting up the distinctions between moralism and religion (VRE, 41–52) and between R_1 and R_2 (VRE, 68–70), and he usually follows them.

A second area of inconsistency concerns the relation between R_1 and the once-born. James's first introduction of the distinction between the once-born and the twice-born occurs at the beginning of his discussion of the religion of healthy-mindedness and seems to imply that adherents of R_1 are once-born (VRE, 73–8). In the passage about Stoicism and Epicureanism quoted in the last paragraph, James seems to identify once-born religion with R_1 and twice-born religion with R_2. Indeed, in another place James explicitly makes this identification. He refers to the "contrast between the two ways of looking at life which are characteristic respectively of what we called the healthy-minded, who need to be born once, and of the sick souls, who must be twice-born in order to be happy" (VRE, 139). But elsewhere and preponderatingly James draws a sharp distinction between adherents of R_1 and the once-born, indicating that R_1 has both once-born and twice-born members. He writes, for example:

> [Mind-curers] have demonstrated that a form of regeneration by relaxing, by letting go, psychologically indistinguishable from the Lutheran justification by faith and the Wesleyan acceptance of free grace, is within the reach of persons who have no conviction of sin and care nothing for the Lutheran theology. (VRE, 96; see also PU, 138)

Even more explicitly, he writes that, in cases of the "mind-cure form of healthy-mindedness, we [find] abundant examples of regenerative process. . . . [I]n many instances it is quite arbitrary whether we class the individual as a once-born or a twice-born subject" (VRE, 385, n. 2).

And in the chapter on the divided self, he quotes at length "an account of [a man's] conversion to the systematic religion of healthy-mindedness" (VRE, 150–2). Although it is tempting to make the facile identification between the once-born and the healthy-minded and between the twice-born and the morbid-minded, most of the textual evidence argues that, while the morbid-minded are of the twice-born type, the healthy-minded may be of either the once-born or the twice-born type.

A third area of inconsistency appears in James's description of R_1 itself. At one point, he writes: "In our future examples, even of the simplest and healthiest-minded type of religious consciousness, we shall find this complex sacrificial constitution, in which a higher happiness holds a lower unhappiness in check" (VRE, 48). But this is inconsistent with numerous passages in which James observes that R_1 is characterized precisely by the pluralistic need to get rid of evil and not to hold it in check as does R_2. For example, he writes that, for R_1: "[Evil] is emphatically irrational, and *not* to be pinned in, or preserved, or consecrated in any final system of truth. It is a pure abomination to the Lord, an alien unreality, a waste element, to be sloughed off and negated, and the very memory of it, if possible, wiped out and forgotten" (VRE, 113; see also 69, 136–8).

A second example of this last area of inconsistency occurs in James's description of the duality in religion. In contrasting healthy-minded with morbid-minded religion, he writes that, for the latter, there are "two lives, the natural and the spiritual, and we must lose the one before we can participate in the other" (VRE, 139). Since James is here contrasting R_1 with R_2, this implies that R_1 does not have these two lives, one of which must be lost to gain the other. But as we have already seen, James elsewhere describes R_1 in just this way when he writes: "The fundamental pillar on which it rests is nothing more than the general basis of all religious experience, the fact that man has a dual nature, and is connected with two spheres of thought, a shallower and a profounder sphere, in either of which he may learn to live more habitually" (VRE, 86).

What are we to make of all these inconsistencies? We might take them as practical applications of James's claim that categories are not so important; that is, as James's attempt to keep his conceptions from being so schematic that they lose all claim to truth.[7] But the fact that the number of contradictions in his description of R_1 is unusually high, even for James, seems to point to a less global explanation. My suggestion is that they are a product of James's attempt, as yet not completely developed, to carve out R_1 as a middle ground between the moralism and the religion he describes in *Literary Remains*. I take this to be the earliest signs of an important shift that occurred in James's thinking toward the end of his life. In chapter 5 we will examine other Jamesian texts that provide further evidence for this shift and that describe its nature and extent in more detail.

Moving beyond the inconsistencies in James's account of healthy-minded religion, it is clear that he believes this religion is quite effective in the practical realm. Its physical, as well as its psychological results, James claims, are far more wide-ranging than most people suspect. Wherever it is effective, James believes, it should be encouraged. But it would be a mistake, he further believes, to assert that healthy-mindedness is effective for all. There are some, whom he calls morbid-minded individuals, for whom healthy-mindedness seems like a hopelessly shallow attempt to escape the reality of evil. It is only to be expected that such individuals would not thrive in healthy-minded religions, but would need morbid-minded religions of their own.

Morbid-Minded Religion (R_2)

Adherents of morbid-minded religion, James says, are very different from adherents of healthy-minded religion. The latter are basically optimistic individuals, who find more goodness and happiness than evil and sadness in life. Morbid-minded individuals, on the other hand, are far more sensitive to the darker side of life. They have lower thresholds of pain, fear, and misery, so it takes smaller amounts of disorder and evil in the physical world to throw their internal, emotional worlds into depression.

An illustration will help draw the contrast James has in mind between healthy-minded and morbid-minded persons. Healthy-minded persons focus on the happiness in life and try to overcome the sadness by getting rid of it or by ignoring it. For them, evil is like a rotten spot in an apple. If you cut this part out and throw it away, you are left with a perfectly good apple. For morbid-minded persons, on the other hand, the sadness in the world vitiates the happiness. For them, evil is more like a chunk of manure in a pail of milk. Removal of the visible impurity does not render the milk fit to drink. For healthy-minded persons, there is a pluralistic rift between good and evil such that, if evil is out of sight, it is out of mind. But the morbid-minded see a monistic connection between the two, so that evil anywhere corrupts happiness everywhere.

It is no wonder that the morbid-minded are quite susceptible to depression. They see evil in the very construction of a universe in which life is predicated on death. They take to heart the fact that it is only the death of certain organisms in this world that makes the life of others possible, and that nowhere is there to be found a life that does not contain the seeds of death. But evil is not limited to the beginning and end of life. At every minute, living things are vulnerable, and they often fall prey to a wide assortment of horrendous diseases and tragedies.

Although the morbid-minded may claim that their pessimism is a result of a realistic and objective view of life, James points out that it is also a function of their emotional and mental constitution. Healthy-minded individuals, even those who are subject to the most cruel experiences, hardly ever reach a morbid-minded level of pessimism and susceptibility to pain. Yet this pessimism and mental anguish are common among the morbid-minded, even among those who have suffered relatively little direct outward tragedy. James claims that this is due both to the higher sensitivity of the morbid-minded and to their neurotic constitution.

James points out that the pathological depression the existence of evil causes in sensitive and neurotic morbid-minded persons can take different forms. It can appear as anhedonia, a condition in which the sufferer is incapable of experiencing joyous feelings. James's example of anhedonia is Tolstoy, who, through a spiritual crisis, came to feel that mortal things are devoid of meaning. The depression can occur as a type of psychical neuralgia, where the sufferer experiences positive and active anguish. James's example is Bunyan, with his intense sense of sin. Worst of all, the depression can take the form of panic fear. James cites his own earlier bout with such panic, which was brought on by a fear of the universe.[8]

In cases of morbid-minded depression, James argues, the healthy-minded cure of minimizing evil by not thinking about it simply does not work. Epicureanism and Stoicism are the best answers the Greeks could give to morbid-minded depression. The Epicurean advice is to avoid unhappiness by giving up intense happiness (since it is always linked to pain) and to avoid disappointment by lowering one's expectations. The Stoic word is to accept the universe outside of ourselves, since it is outside of our control. The only things we can control are our attitudes and emotions. To do so well is the only real good in life. For James, these Epicurean and Stoic doctrines are not so much cures as ways of hunkering down and trying to bear the disease.

The message of morbid-minded religions, such as Buddhism, Christianity, Hinduism, and Islam, is paradoxical. It is that happiness is to be found, neither through trying to minimize evil nor through trying to learn to bear it, but through maximizing our feeling of it. Thus, if understood correctly, the neurotic constitution and the pathological nature of the morbid-minded are the means of their salvation. It is because of them that the pain is intensified to such a degree that a conversion can occur that, paradoxically, takes the sting out of the pain.

Taking a close look at James's views on conversion is helpful for understanding his view of religion; even more important for present purposes, it is crucial for understanding the metaphysical self. We will find that the subconscious, which plays a vital role in conversion, is a principal point of connection in the divine–human nexus that constitutes religion. Understanding James's use of the subconscious is thus crucial for understanding the relation between the human self and the divine self. There is another level of complexity, as well, that is opened up by a proper understanding of the role of the subconscious in James's thought. The relation between the conscious self and its subconscious is similar to that between the human self and the divine. Understanding the connection between the conscious self and its subconscious as described by James in the conversion process here will prepare us for moving to James's discussion of the relation between the human self and the divine self in *A Pluralistic Universe*.

Conversion

James defines conversion as the process "by which a self hitherto divided, and consciously wrong or unhappy, becomes unified and consciously right superior and happy, in consequence of its firmer hold upon religious realities" (VRE, 157). But conversion is "only one species of a genus that contains other types as well." James goes on to cite other species of this unnamed genus: "For example, the new birth may be away from religion into incredulity; or it may be from moral scrupulosity into freedom and license; or it may be produced by the irruption into the individual's life of some new stimulus or passion, such as love, ambition, cupidity, revenge, or patriotic devotion" (VRE, 146).

Conversion, for James, can result in inner unity and peace in different ways: "It may come gradually, or it may come abruptly; it may come through altered feelings, or through altered powers of action; or it may come through new intellectual insights, or through experiences which we shall later have to designate as 'mystical' " (VRE, 146). However it may occur, James maintains, its result is sometimes the resolution of a problem all of us have in one degree or another as adolescents (VRE, 164–6). Our personalities are initially a rather chaotic mixture of noble and common desires and healthy and harmful impulses from which a stable character must evolve if we are to be at peace with ourselves. In the case of heterogeneous or discordant personalities, where the initial character is unusually chaotic, the search for and the attainment of this inner peace through conversion is especially common.

James contends, as we have seen, that conversion is a common element of both R_1 and R_2. In R_1 it is achieved through minimizing evil, whereas in R_2 it is experienced by maximizing evil. R_1 conversion results in the radical elimination of evil from the field of consciousness, whereas R_2 conversion retains the serious presence of evil, but takes away its sting. Despite these differences, R_1 and R_2 conversions have similar functions, are indistinguishable psychologically (VRE, 96), and by means of the union with the divine to which they lead, have the same practical significance for the individual (VRE, 385, n. 2).

Because each of us must play a variety of roles in life, James argues, it is healthy for the normal individual to have different ideas and aims associated with each of the roles. The President of the United States acts differently when on vacation than when in the Oval Office. We act differently when at a baseball game than when visiting a friend in the hospital. We usually move in and out of these roles with ease. Moments of levity give way to moments of responsibility and seriousness and then claim our attention again. What seems "hot and vital" today seems cold and unimportant tomorrow. In heterogeneous personalities, however, there is a "great oscillation in the emotional interests, and the hot places . . . shift before one almost as rapidly as the sparks that run through burnt-up paper" (VRE, 162). Conversion can arrest this vacillation—often in a sudden way—when one single religious point of view comes to stable domination in a previously heterogeneous personality.

James holds that conversion, especially in its more sudden and violent instantiations, is largely a result of the subconscious processing of experience. As we get older, new experience tends to call for a shift in our center of energy, whereas habits that we have developed tend to keep us at the old center. When this happens, our habits normally shift to keep up with the new experience. Sometimes, however, deeply entrenched habits may keep us acting in accordance with the old center of energy long after our subconscious selves have actually shifted away from it. In this case, some event, trivial or important, may serve to jar us from the old center to the new one without a sufficient conscious explanation for the shift. Understandably, experiences of this sort often seem like miraculous conversions to those who experience them.

James believes that at least many of these conversions can be explained in terms of the convert's susceptibility to subconscious influences. He hails the discovery of the subconscious, or the subliminal self, as the most important discovery in psychology since he began his studies in the field (VRE, 190). This discovery shows that the conscious selves of which we are aware are surrounded by a whole mass of our memories, latent impulses, and powers of which we are not aware. He points out, however, that it is impossible to draw the boundary between the conscious and the subconscious with absolute precision. Thus, it is often unclear whether or not we are actually conscious of particular thoughts.

In some temperaments, James observes, the subconscious region is especially large and the boundary between it and the conscious region especially pervious. In these cases more than in others, work can go on unnoticed in the subconscious and then burst into the conscious realm, suddenly upsetting the conscious equilibrium. In other temperaments, James argues, the subconscious region is not so fertile, and the conscious self is not so open to its suggestions. Persons with these temperaments are not very likely candidates for instantaneous conversion.

James suggests that the reason certain persons have experienced instantaneous conversions and others have not is a function, not of the presence or absence of divine grace, but of a temperamental difference on the part of the converts. Persons with strong emotional sensibility, a tendency toward automatisms, and a great degree of passive suggestibility are more likely than others to experience instantaneous conversion. Persons without such characteristics in their personalities, if they are converted at all, will likely experience gradual conversions.

What is the value of sudden conversions? To answer this question, James looks at the fruits of such experiences. They often result in dramatic and permanent changes for the better in the lives of the converts. But it does not follow that all such converts live better lives than all of those who have not been converted in this way. In fact, James points out, in all levels of spiritual maturity, there are those with and those without such conversion experiences. So, as James sees it, it is not justifiable to hold instantaneous conversion to be an experience that everyone must have to be truly religious. Nor is it justifiable, he argues, to accept such experiences as a complete confirmation of the doctrinal positions of the converts, especially because these positions are often contradictory. What *is* justifiable, for James, is to conclude that those who are capable of having such experiences should be encouraged in them, since they seem for the most part to make converts' lives better than they otherwise would be.

It would, however, be a mistake to think of James as being in agreement with his colleagues in psychology who hold that conversions are merely natural occurrences with natural causes. While James does maintain that psychological descriptions can go a long way toward helping us understand natural subconscious processes, he goes on to argue that some conversions are so sudden and have so little evidence of subconscious incubation that it seems they must be influenced either physiologically, through some sort of epileptic episode, or else, as he believes of at least some cases, supernaturally, through divine intervention. Furthermore, James points out, subconscious incubation does not rule out the possibility of divine influence. It may be that God communicates with our subconscious in a way analogous to the method by which our subconscious communicates with our conscious self.

With these possibilities in mind, we are ready to move from James's empirical study of religious experience in *Varieties* to the metaphysical account of what James believes lies behind those experiences in *A Pluralistic Universe*. In this latter work, we will find a radical exposition of the metaphysical self that presupposes much of James's discussion in *Varieties*, but that also moves beyond that discussion toward the resolution of much of the tension we have found in it.

A PLURALISTIC UNIVERSE

In formulating his religious over-beliefs in *A Pluralistic Universe*, James is consciously proceeding beyond the realm of contemporary scientific discovery. We have already seen, in chapter 1, James's answer to those who claim that such moves are illegitimate. He argues that individuals have the right to decide genuine options that cannot be decided intellectually in accordance with their passional nature. James is here exercising that right. In examining the field of living hypotheses, James finds three that attempt to explain the nature of God and his relation to the human self: theism, absolute idealism, and James's own radical empiricism.

Three Disjunctions

James presents these three hypotheses by means of three disjunctions. The first disjunction is between materialistic and spiritualistic philosophies. James says very little about materialistic philosophies, since none of his living options is materialistic. He points out that these philosophies hold our souls to be alien to the world. They do not allow us to be intimate with the world, since they hold that the more primary and lasting things in it are foreign to us. Consequently, they require us to be perpetually wary, tense, and on guard. James observes that only persons of cynical temperament hold such views and that few people are cynics because they like cynicism. Instead, most cynics have adopted cynicism either because they think the facts force them to this view or because they are reacting to the extreme tender-mindedness of idealism. Because most people are of a sympathetic temperament, they hold to spiritualistic philosophies. According to these philosophies, the intimate and human is primary to the "brutal" and "foreign" in the universe (PU, 19). This means that we can trust and embrace the universe and need have no ultimate fear of it.

James's second disjunction is that spiritualistic philosophies are either theistic or pantheistic. James claims that theism, which he iden-tifies as the first living hypothesis, defines God principally as the external creator.[9] The universe is dualistic, consisting of God and his creation, with the creation further divided into nature and human beings. Although God is conscious and personal, he is also totally other and independent from us. The relation between God and his creation is radically asymmetrical. God's action affects the creation, but God can never be affected by the creation's reaction. God's being and nature mean that truth is complete and that it is established inde-pendently of us. Our place is merely to acknowledge it and to live our lives in accordance with it.

Pantheism, James argues, denies the separation between human beings and God by claiming that we are essentially one with God. The pantheistic God is not an external creator, but the internal divine spark in each of us. Thus, for pantheism, we all form one continuous soul and body with God. But there are different kinds of pantheisms, and in his third and final disjunction, James identifies absolute idealism and radical empiricism as the two kinds that form the second and third living hypotheses.

Absolute idealism, or the philosophy of the Absolute as James calls it, is a monistic pantheism. That is, it considers the whole to be primary to the parts. The divine and the human are one, but are fully divine only in the form of totality. This totality, the Absolute, is nothing but the knowledge of objects, and objects are nothing but what the Absolute knows. Philosophers belong to this objective realm. The Ab-solute makes us by thinking us and becomes conscious of itself through

our thoughts. From the perspective of the Absolute, the world is perfect. It is only our limited perspective as a part of that world that gives
rise to mistakes, curiosity, and pain.

James's radical empiricism does not privilege the whole over the
parts. It is satisfied with the possibility that there may never be an
"all-form" of the universe at all. The "each-form," which is the way
we humans experience the world, is sufficient. Radical empiricism
holds that God is also one of the each-forms. Thus, radical empiricism
can be described as pluralistic in form, although not in substance. That
is, it is pluralistic in that it claims reality may never be formed into one
single totality, but it is not pluralistic in that it claims we are substantially one with God. Paradoxically, yet accurately, James describes
radical empiricism as a "pluralistic pantheism."

To James and his Oxford audience, theism is the least attractive
of the three living hypotheses. Consequently, he makes fairly short
work of it, in terms of the previous critique. James's main goal in this
series of lectures is to attack the idealism so prevalent at Oxford at the
time and to defend his own radical empiricism. Accordingly, James
examines idealism and radical empiricism in greater detail. It is important to follow this examination closely, since it contains much that
is of importance for understanding James's move toward the integration of the individual self.

Absolute Idealism

James's critique of idealism includes two separate attacks. First, he
argues against the claim that it is necessarily true. Second, he argues
that, because of internal contradictions and its inability to satisfy our
religious needs, it is not even probably true.

James identifies four steps in the process by which idealists try
to show that their doctrine is necessarily true. First, idealists presuppose that the world must be rational and self-consistent. Second, since
the experienced world of sense-data is an unacceptably chaotic flux,
they substitute a conceptual world for the perceptual one. Third, they
interpret the conceptual world intellectualistically, so that its concepts
offer no continuity with which to replace the perceptual continuity
native to sense-experience. Finally, because this state of affairs is intol-
erable, they postulate the Absolute to bring unity to the radical conceptual discontinuity. As a result of this process, idealists such as Lotze,
Royce, and Bradley conclude that any independence between things
in the universe leads to chaos and that any dependence at all among
them leads to identity.

James argues against this process at every step. First, he contends that the world is not rational and self-consistent. This reflects an important shift in James's thinking. It clears the way for his acceptance of the metaphysical compounding of consciousness, a point to which we will return later in this chapter. Second, although James admits that concepts are rational and serve a quite useful practical purpose, he rejects the notion that they are the means whereby we come to know the reality of the world. James holds, on the contrary, that the substitution of a conceptual order for the perceptual one is a move away from, not toward, ultimate reality. As for the third step in the idealist argument, James labels this intellectualistic treatment of concepts "vicious intellectualism." He understands vicious intellectualism to be "the treating of a name as excluding from the fact named what the name's definition fails positively to include" (PU, 32, italics deleted). James points out that the application of this principle leads to such palpable absurdities as the conclusion that a person, once having been named an equestrian, can never in the future exhibit the characteristics of a pedestrian (PU, 32). James holds that the fourth step, the introduction of what he calls the "absolute *deus ex machina*" (PU, 38), is rendered unnecessary by the rejection of the first three steps. He argues further that the Absolute is not only unnecessary, but also irrational.

Turning to Hegel, James contends that his vision is, in many ways, quite insightful and valuable but that the technical apparatus through which he tries to work out his vision is not. Hegel's vision is that reason is all-inclusive, that reason is able to overcome the superficial irrationality in appearances by taking it up as a moment into itself. James admits that Hegel's dialectic, which James includes as a part of his vision, shows Hegel to be quite sensitive to the nature of the empirical flux of experience. But Hegel's technique, according to James, is a miserable failure. He points out that even Hegel's disciples, for the most part, reject all of his particular applications of his method. His terrible style and his deliberate vagueness and ambiguity contribute, according to James, to the failure of his technique. So great is this failure, to James's mind, that he considers Hegel to be "one of those numerous original seers who can never learn how to articulate" (PU, 53). Although James is tempted by Hegel's rationalistic vision because of its promise of intimacy with the universe, he ultimately rejects it in favor of pluralism. This is not because he gives up his hope of intimacy, but because he finds another way of obtaining it—a way that does not jar so much with his need for meaning.

James is more favorably disposed toward the dialectical part of Hegel's vision. He calls Hegel's transformation of the category of negation his most original stroke (PU, 47). He agrees with Hegel's observation that things pass over into their own others. Finite things are not independent, but are essentially related to other things. James believes that this insight would be developed best by means of an empirical logic. Hegel chooses, instead, to develop a rationalism that leaves concrete things to one side in favor of the concepts substituted for them. This leads, according to James, to a vicious intellectualism, where a thing's finitude is interpreted as a negation of all other things. James argues that this vicious intellectualism requires Hegel to postulate an Absolute that can restore the unity of things by taking up all finite things into itself.

Since James holds that reality is primarily perceptual and not conceptual, he concludes that the doctrine of the Absolute is not, contrary to what idealists claim, absolutely true. For James, reality carries with it its own continuity, and is not in need of external unification. In fact, James argues that there is a sense in which, if things are taken empirically and not intellectualistically, they can be seen to be their own others in a way similar to that in which Hegel claims the Absolute to be its own other.

If absolute idealism is not necessarily true, is it probably true? Although James is not convinced of the Absolute by means of Hegel's technical apparatus, he is certainly tempted by it on the basis of its practical religious effects. At least for people of certain temperaments, belief in the Absolute can create a deep religious peace. Some people find a deep contentment in the knowledge that, at the highest level—which is absolute and unchanging—all is right with the universe. Although this is a valuable practical effect of absolute idealism, James argues against its acceptance because of other practical failures.

Perhaps the greatest practical failure of the Absolute is its inability to solve the problem of evil. James makes much of the difficulty of accounting for the presence of evil in an idealist universe. At the level of the Absolute, there is, of course, no evil. But it is hard to see, James argues, how the Absolute can be an ideally perfect whole, when most, if not all, of its parts are so imperfect. It is not as if the perfection of the whole were dependent on the existence of the imperfect parts, since idealism claims that the whole is primary to its parts. Furthermore, it is a mystery why there are conscious parts of the universe at all, particularly when these parts seem to be necessarily surrounded by the evil that is a function of their finitude. It seems easy to imagine an ideal whole more perfect than the Absolute—a whole, for example, in which there are no imperfect parts.

A second problem with the Absolute, James argues, is that it is useless for deductive purposes. Because it has no predictive power whatsoever, it is good for helping to explain only what has already happened. This means, for one thing, that it is useless for science.

A third problem James has with the Absolute can perhaps be most easily stated in terms of the problem the young Socrates had to face with respect to ideas in the *Parmenides*. Just as the Platonic doctrine of ideas seems to require there to be ideas for silly things such as "hair, mud, and dirt,"[10] so the doctrine of the Absolute can account for the existence of silly and nonsensical ideas only by their having been thought by the Absolute.

James's conclusion from these arguments is that the claim that the Absolute exists is neither necessarily nor probably true. He makes it clear, however, that the failure of the Absolute does not leave us without recourse for the employment of our religious will to believe. It is possible to disbelieve in the existence of the Absolute without giving up all belief in superhuman consciousness. James discusses the metaphysical views of Gustav Fechner as one example of this possibility. It is through the Fechnerian worldview that James turns to the elaboration of his own radical empiricism.

Radical Empiricism

Fechner is a panpsychist who believes in the compounding of consciousness.[11] As a panpsychist, he holds that each part of the universe is conscious. That is, consciousness is common not only to humans, but also to animals and plants and rocks. With respect to the compounding of consciousness, he holds that aggregates of these conscious parts of the universe can be conscious, as well. He argues that, just as our various sense-perceptions are separate entities that are compounded in our consciousnesses, so the consciousnesses inherent in all things can be compounded in higher minds. For example, the consciousnesses of individual human beings are constituents of the consciousness of the human race. The human and animal consciousnesses are constituents of a larger consciousness, which, in turn, joins with the consciousness of the plant kingdom to form the consciousness of the earth soul. But this compounding, according to Fechner, is not merely terrestrial. The consciousness of the earth soul contributes to the consciousness of the solar system, which, in turn, contributes to still greater consciousnesses, all of which contribute to the consciousness of God, the mind of the universe.

James admits that Fechner's postulation of God as the supreme consciousness of the universe reveals him to be a monist on the speculative level. Although James is an avowed enemy of monism, there are several reasons why he is not overly concerned by Fechner's monism.

First, James argues that Fechner is not a monist at the practical level, since, on this level, he deals almost exclusively with the earth soul. Second, James points out that Fechner does not give a very detailed definition of God, leaving him vague and abstract. James concludes that this God probably functions for Fechner merely as a way of limiting what would otherwise be an infinite hierarchy of deities. Finally, James believes that even this abstract, speculative monism is not logically required by Fechner's other views.

On the practical level, Fechner holds the earth soul to be a sort of guardian angel, to which human beings may pray. If it is true that the earth has a consciousness, he argues, this consciousness must be superior to ours. After all, the earth has a greater independence, a greater complexity in unity, a more extensive internal development as opposed to formation from without, and a higher degree of difference from other beings of its type.

The earth soul also functions for Fechner as the guarantor of personal immortality. Just as a visual sense-datum is taken up into our human brains and remains there, both in its particularity and in society with other data and thoughts, even after the eyes are closed or cease to function, so, according to Fechner, our distinct, individual contribution to the earth soul continues after our death.

James's favorable presentation of Fechner's views notwithstanding, it would be a mistake to think that he accepts them as literally true. Although James is careful to present Fechner in a positive light, a bit of reflection reveals that Fechner's views are open to too many objections, including ones very similar to those James levies against absolute idealism, for James to take them at face value. First, Fechner's views do not solve the problem of evil. If the earth is our guardian angel, it is a poor one. Despite its guardianship, the human mortality rate is one hundred percent. In fact, it is the earth that harbors and nourishes the diseases that prove debilitating and fatal to us. Nor, in spite of our prayers, does it deliver us from the many other sorts of evils that beset us.[12] Second, Fechner's analogical system seems fantastic. What things would be barred by it from being constituents of a single consciousness? Perhaps I, along with my desk, computer, and books, constitute an office consciousness greater than its parts. Going further, we find the same problem here that Parmenides had with the doctrine of forms and that James has with absolute idealism—namely, silliness. Might not all the mud in the world form a single consciousness? Or perhaps there exists somewhere a consciousness whose constituents are a New York taxi driver, a Mexican donkey, and a certain silkworm in China.

If Fechner's views are not to be taken literally, why does James discuss them in *A Pluralistic Universe*? James answers this question himself. More than once, James says he introduces Fechner because of the richness of his description. His intention is to "thicken up" metaphysical debate, which to his mind was being carried out in a very thin way by contemporary idealists (PU, 81, 149). When James complains that the debate is "thin," he means that it is being carried out in accordance with what he sees as unimaginative and abstract intellectualist views that are far from the percepts in which he believes the debate should be rooted. James also has a "much deeper reason" for discussing Fechner. It is his way of introducing the problem of the compounding of consciousness (PU, 81–2).

Metaphysical views like Fechner's presuppose that consciousness can be compounded. That is, they assume that states of consciousness "can separate and combine themselves freely, and keep their own identity unchanged while forming parts of simultaneous fields of experience of wider scope" (PU, 83). Viewed from the top down, the assumption is of collective experiences "claiming identity with their constituent parts, yet experiencing things quite differently from these latter" (PU, 93). The psychological version of this theory, the mind-dust theory, claims that complex states of mind arise from the self-compounding of "primordial units of mind-stuff or mind-dust" (PU, 85). James cites his argument against this theory in *Principles*, where he has opted instead for a pluralism, "treating each total field of consciousness as a distinct entity, and maintaining that the higher fields merely supersede the lower functionally by knowing more about the same objects" (PU, 92; see PP, 148–82).

Until a few years before delivering the Hibbert Lectures, James admits, he would have argued that the compounding of consciousness is impossible metaphysically as well as psychologically. But James now recognizes that his earlier position leads to a radical discontinuity between mental states, since it entails that mental states of various levels of complexity have no being in common. If they have no being in common, there can be no subjective communication between them. This subjective isolation cannot be overcome by pointing to the unity of the object, since it is hard to see how a single object could appear so different in various mental states. Because of its differing appearances, the objective world falls apart into discontinuous bits just as radically as the subjective one does.

In trying to overcome this radical discontinuity, James faces a trilemma similar to the one among the three living metaphysical hypotheses with which he begins the lectures. The only way this discontinuity can be overcome, James maintains, is by accepting the existence of souls, by giving up the logic of identity, or by admitting that human experience is fundamentally irrational. Theism holds to the existence of souls, and absolute idealism gives up the logic of identity in favor of a higher, dialectical logic. James adopts the third alternative and gives it the name of radical empiricism. In general, radical empiricism is James's term for the notion that everything in experience is real. In the present context, James describes radical empiricism as holding human experience to be fundamentally irrational, or, if one prefers, fundamentally nonrational. James is willing to accept either term. His claim is simply, "Reality, life, experience, concreteness, immediacy, use what word you will, exceeds our logic, overflows and surrounds it" (PU, 96).

In chapter 5, we will take up in more detail James's discussion of the relation between concrete experience and logic. It is enough for my present purpose to summarize the results of this discussion. James concludes that—although static, conceptual logic is of great practical and, within certain limits, theoretical value—the real world of being is a rich and continuous world in constant flux. Concrete experiences contain within them their own perceptual relations. In short, reality is "synechistic";[13] it is a continuum, where identifying a discrete member of the continuum entails breaking the continuum at that point (PU, 146–7).

We have seen that, in *Principles*, James describes consciousness as a stream of thought (PP, 233). In *A Pluralistic Universe*, he expands that description, seeing reality itself to be a great stream of being. It is no longer merely consciousness that is a continuum containing its own relations. Now reality itself contains its own relations in a stream where both the parts and the wholes form a sort of heterogeneous continuum.[14]

Although mental states cannot be logically compounded in the world of abstract concepts, James claims that they *are* actually compounded in the stream of being. Here, mental facts do function both individually and with others at the same time, and their functioning together no more changes their individual nature than the nature of a bodily sensation is changed by moving from our subconscious to our consciousness.

James concludes that neither absolutism nor radical empiricism is rendered impossible on the basis of the presupposition of the self-compounding of consciousness. Because he has already rejected absolute idealism on grounds other than its reliance on self-compounding, radical empiricism is left as the final living hypothesis. In our discussion of conversion, we noted James's view that each human mind is composed of a conscious center that shades off gradually into the subconscious. In a similar way, radical empiricism holds that each human mind functions as a single mental fact for itself, while at the same time shading off into a larger consciousness of which it is a constitutive part. For James it is precisely the notion that the individual is constitutive of this larger consciousness that safeguards the integrity of the individual. Thus, even with James's acceptance of the self-compounding of consciousness, his individualism is more thoroughgoing—as we shall see in chapter 5—than that of other nineteenth-century individualists.

James argues that a further strength of radical empiricism is its ability to account for religious experience. He contends that religious experience, including conversion, cannot be sufficiently explained by psychology and that such experience argues for the continuity of our consciousness with a larger spiritual world. As further evidence of this continuity, James cites cases of split human personality, as well as the phenomena of automatic writing and speech and of mediumship and possession. Of the three ways to interpret this evidence—that is, of the three living hypotheses described earlier—James argues that the path of least resistance is provided by the pluralistic pantheism of radical empiricism.

James approves of Fechner's description of a "great reservoir in which memories of earth's inhabitants are pooled and preserved, and from which, when the threshold lowers or the valve opens, information ordinarily shut out leaks into the mind of exceptional individuals among us" (PU, 135). Along with his approval, however, James contends that the details of this superhuman reservoir must be kept "very vague" and that the number of individuals whose memories it preserves must be left open (PU, 140).

Pluralistic pantheism does insist on one important detail about this reservoir. In order to avoid responsibility for the existence of evil, God must be finite. God must be finite in his power or in his knowledge, or both. James points out that this has been the normal view of God in common religion (PU, 141). This point casts further light on James's description of radical empiricism as a pluralistic pantheism. Because James argues that the universe is pantheistic in substance, but pluralistic in form, this means that human beings may be substantially one with God, but that God's form is not infinite. Since God constitutes only the ideal part of the universe, evil is excluded from the divine reservoir.

With this presentation of James's vague yet important over-beliefs about God, we come to the end of our examination of his view of the metaphysical self. We have followed James's discussion from his analysis of religious experience to his examination of the subconscious, which he suggests is the nexus between the divine realm and the human individual. Following the analogy between the conscious self and the subconscious in human experience, we then moved beyond the subconscious to James's discussion of the larger spiritual world surrounding it. We also noted the tension that appears in various places, especially in James's discussions in *Varieties*. Comparing the perceptual individualism we explored in this chapter with the volitional individualism James earlier espoused only increases the tension. Our first task in the next chapter will be to work toward the resolution of this tension. This will lead to a discussion in the following chapter of the integrated self and the presentation of the mature Jamesian individualism to which it gives rise. At that point, the diachronic and organic nature of James's dynamic individualism will be much more clearly visible.

PART II

An Interpretation of the Dynamic Individualism of William James

CHAPTER 4

Methods of Interpreting James

In the previous three chapters, we have engaged in a detailed examination of James's writings on individualism. Because of his piecemeal treatment of the topic, this has required the examination of a wide variety of his works. To this point, we have rarely strayed from a close analysis of the texts in which James discusses the relation of an individual to other individuals, the psychological constitution of the individual, and the religious and metaphysical dimensions of the individual. Our analysis of these texts has laid the groundwork for the final three chapters in this book. Although some textual work remains to be done, we are now free to take a broader look at James's views.

Our task in Part II is an interpretation of James's individualism. This does not mean that we will arrive at a single, clear picture of this aspect of James's thought. This would not only be nearly impossible, given the complexity of his views, but it would also mean doing violence to the gothic spirit of his philosophy. For James, too much neatness and precision in a theory, too many clear-cut categories, are sure signs of intellectualistic tampering with reality. James finds clear-cut, rationalistic architectonics not only inaccurate to the pluralistic complexity of the world, but flat and sterile, as well. Any theory that purports to be Jamesian must not do violence to James's pluralistic vision.

Still, pluralism is not confusion, and the tension in James's various discussions of individualism is too great to be ignored. This tension is due partly to the fact that James's colorful and captivating style is often far from precise. Added to this vagueness, moreover, is a large number of inconsistencies that appear, not only from one work to another, but sometimes also within the same book. A further challenge is presented by the fact that the texts I have examined on individualism were written by James over a span of almost thirty years. His discussion of the individual in "Reflex Action and Theism," a lecture delivered in 1881, is significantly different from his discussion of it in *A Pluralistic Universe*, a series of lectures delivered in 1908 and 1909. The vaguenesses, inconsistencies, and changes in James's work are not limited to his discussions of individualism. They are pervasive problems that confront any reader of Jamesian texts. Before we can proceed further in our understanding of James's individualism, we must address the question of how these vaguenesses, inconsistencies, and changes in James's work are to be understood. Various commentators have suggested a number of explanations for the tensions in James's work. In this chapter, we will examine some of those explanations, noting their advantages and disadvantages. In the next chapter, I will present my Integration Thesis and show how this constitutes an important new way of understanding some of these tensions.

TWO CAMPS

On the issue of interpreting vaguenesses, inconsistencies, and changes in James's work, Charlene Haddock Seigfried divides commentators into two basic camps. She writes:

> The secondary literature on James is divided on whether his writings are best grasped as a series of brilliant insights, their very disconnectedness being seen as evidence of his anti-rationalistic, anti-systematic, anti-foundationalist stances, or whether his writings form a unified whole, even though the coherence has to be sought despite often contrary appearances.[1]

Beginning with this basic division, we can make an even finer distinction within each of the two basic camps. Those who hold James's writings to be best characterized as antisystematic can be further divided as to whether they think the inconsistencies in James's texts are accidental or intentional. Those who hold James's writings to be basically coherent can be further divided into those who find a basic unity in the texts and those who find in them a deep duality. A look at the views of a few representative commentators will make these further divisions more clear.

Some commentators try to explain the abundance of textual difficulties in James by characterizing him as a thinker like they take Rousseau or Emerson to be, a thinker bursting with too many insights to be overly concerned about their consistent presentation. According to this view, vagueness, inconsistency, and change in James's work are functions of a lack of clarity in his own mind and a carelessness in the exposition of his thoughts. Charles Peirce was an early critic whose views support this interpretation of James. Although Peirce admired James's ability to arrive at the right answers and to communicate these answers to others, he complained to James of what he saw as a careless or untrained lack of clarity. It was only when James wrote in French, Peirce claimed, and was "tied down to the rules of French rhetoric" that he wrote clearly enough for Peirce to understand what he meant (CWJ, 11:568). After having received a copy of James's *Pragmatism*, Peirce even went so far as to offer to give James a crash course in learning to "think with more exactitude" (CWJ, 11:612–3).

There is certainly some truth to Peirce's complaints. It is sometimes quite frustrating to try to work out clearly what James thinks about a certain issue. Going below the surface of James's gripping style and powerful rhetoric all too often leads to bewilderment. In the last chapter, I pointed out an example of this in some detail. I argued that the inconsistencies in James's discussion of moralism, healthy-minded religion, and morbid-minded religion indicate that James is not entirely clear in his own mind about the various distinctions he wants to make. It would, however, be unfair to James to interpret all of these textual problems as merely cases of "slap-dash" thinking.[2]

Frederick Ruf sees at least many of these apparent contradictions in James's work as intentional. Ruf points out that James is fond of sketching and suggesting and argues that much of what appears contradictory on a discursive level is profoundly rich on a less literal level. For Ruf, James's style is necessary to produce the richness in his work. Ruf argues further that the apparent confusion in James's work is a carefully planned rhetorical reinforcement of his pluralistic message. James uses chaos to create a world in which falsely grounded and wooden beliefs can be disordered.

Similar in many respects to Ruf's view is that advanced by William Joseph Gavin. Gavin takes seriously James's claim in *Principles* that "It is, in short, the re-instatement of the vague to its proper place in our mental life which I am so anxious to press on the attention" (PP, 246). Gavin emphasizes James's rejection of the view that reality is fully given to us in concepts. He points out that James believes both in the inadequacy of concepts and in their necessity. Indeed, Gavin's position is borne out when we turn to *A Pluralistic Universe*. James there writes that concepts are the result of a process of "translating the crude flux of our merely feeling-experience into a conceptual order" (PU, 98). But James is clear to point out that this conceptual order is only an "inadequate second," never the "full equivalent" of the original perceptual flux (PU, 118; see also SPP, 45–7). This means that the attempt to reconstruct reality on the basis of concepts will be forever frustrated.[3]

James uses Zeno's Paradox of Achilles and the Tortoise to show the inadequacy of conceptual interpretations of perception. In the paradox, motion inherent in perception is translated into static concepts. The result of this translation is that the conceptual understanding of the event does not match the perceptual experience of it. James's conclusion from this paradox is exactly the opposite of Zeno's. Whereas Zeno concludes that perception is illusory, James concludes that reality is not rational. That is, reality does not yield itself entirely to conceptualization.

On James's view, conceptualization fails in three ways. First, the conceptual representation of percepts will never be completely accurate. All translations fall short. Second, because perceptual reality is always in flux, it can never be fully captured by static concepts. In making this point, Gavin labels James's position "radical realism," since he holds that reality "is not coextensive with the knowable."[4] Third, some concepts will contradict others. The acceptance of this third failure amounts to a rejection of rationalism. Rationalists have traditionally held that the coherence of concepts with each other is more important than their correspondence with percepts. To this, James gives an empiricist reply that reality is in the realm of percepts. Thus, it is more important that concepts correspond to percepts as accurately as possible than that they cohere with other concepts. This is not to say that concepts are unimportant. James points out their usefulness in helping us think through problems and reach goals. We must simply realize that, valuable though it is, conceptual clarification is never infallible. It is crucial that we lose sight neither of its importance nor of its imperfection.

James's view of conceptualization might be used to explain the tension present in his thought. Just as Aristotle would hold it unwise to expect geometrical precision in the study of ethics, so James claims it is a mistake to expect univocal clarity in the conceptual realm. Difficulties in James's texts would then properly be assigned to the failure of conceptualization.

Given this failure of conceptualization, and by implication of language, Gavin sees James's texts as indispensable attempts to accomplish the impossible. Caught in the irony of the need for trying to understand reality conceptually at the same time that he understands the impossibility of doing so, James uses his texts as a spur to point to what cannot be said. Gavin writes:

> [James's] texts constitute a spur... an invitation to "overcome" them by going further, in application and in conversation. There is, then, still something "ineffable" or "inarticulate" about the texts written by James, something "more," in that they undermine themselves, indirectly disclose their own insufficiency, urge the reader to "surpass" them. . . .[5]

Peirce, Ruf, and Gavin are each right in some measure. Their methods of interpretation are valuable as far as they go. They provide important insights into understanding much of the vagueness, inconsistency, and change in James's texts. Although Ruf and Gavin are correct in pointing out the intentional nature of chaos and vagueness in James's work, they leave us with too much of this chaos and vagueness. They each suggest ways of understanding why the textual difficulties are present in James's work more than they do ways of resolving those difficulties. But not all methods of interpreting James's work take the difficulties for granted. Some point out ways of eliminating them, or, at least, of minimizing them.

Ellen Kappy Suckiel argues that "as a philosopher James was far more careful and systematic than he led his readers to believe." She acknowledges that James was "frequently contradictory" and that it is difficult to trace in his work a "clear and coherent philosophy." But she argues that this is due to the fact that James's "most influential writings appear in the form of semipopular lectures." Instead of the painstaking articulation of his views and their unification in a systematized whole that we might expect from a technical philosopher, James uses a more imaginative and dramatic style of expression he deemed rhetorically appropriate for the specific audiences for whom his lectures were intended. But Suckiel wants to distinguish between the mode of presentation of James's ideas and his very careful deliberation about them. If we peer beneath James's frequently problematic rhetorical articulations, Suckiel suggests, we will find a coherent philosophical vision. "This vision, whatever its difficulties, is the result of a consistent philosophical methodology, the elements of which relate in sophisticated and conceptually integrated ways." Suckiel's goal is "ultimately to establish the value of [James's] pragmatism as a technical and systematic philosophy."[6]

It might be instructive to consider one example of how Suckiel applies her views to a particular problem in James's texts. When discussing James's view of truth in religion, Suckiel carefully examines his pragmatic position and defends it against the charge of subjectivism. Then she notes that in various places in *The Will to Believe* and in *Varieties*, James seems to espouse a realist position. In those passages, she observes, James "makes a point of *distinguishing* the truth of religious and metaphysical propositions from the beneficial consequences of believing them."[7] In the face of this apparent contradiction, Suckiel refuses to side with those interpreters who simply conclude that James "did not place a high value on consistency." Instead, she suggests that, in *The Will to Believe*, James is making the important rhetorical move of provisionally accepting the views of the members of his audience. No damage is ultimately done to James's views, for Suckiel, because he goes on to show that these realist views are irrelevant for questions of practical religious belief. James's discussion in *Varieties*, Suckiel contends further, emphasizes the importance of the empirical confirmability of religious belief. But because, for James, this confirmability takes place within—and not outside of—experience, it does not commit him to a realist position after all. Instead of accepting an apparent contradiction in James at face value, then, Suckiel looks for ways of getting beneath the rhetoric to a systematic and coherent position.

Seigfried, too, weighs in on the side of those who see an "inner coherence" in James's work. Although she points out the dangers of trying to force James's writings too neatly into a "false conformity," she argues for a developmental view of James's thinking. She organizes this development around three major crises she sees in James's life and thought. The first crisis is the famous depression he went through in his late twenties, the second involves his development of the pragmatic method as a way of integrating science and metaphysics, and the third is constituted by his rejection of "intellectualistic logic" in favor of a "pluralistic rejection of one all-encompassing explanatory system."[8]

Wesley Cooper also finds an inner coherence in James's work. But he sees a fundamental duality in that inner coherence. In his recent book *The Unity of William James's Thought*, he tries to minimize difficulties in James's texts by separating James's scientific writings from his metaphysical ones. He argues that the two resulting sets of writings are internally consistent, although they are not necessarily consistent with each other. Cooper calls his thesis the "Two-Levels

View." He claims: "The Two-Levels View... distinguishes scientific and metaphysical levels of James's system, minimizing contradiction and maximizing plausibility within it by showing how apparently conflicting claims can cohere by limiting their scope to one or the other of the two levels."[9] Cooper points out that James has been interpreted in very different and conflicting ways—as a neutral monist, a naturalistic physicalist, a panpsychist, and a phenomenologist—and argues that his thesis helps reconcile these interpretations by showing at what level and to what extent each holds true.

As we have already seen, Bixler, too, tries to minimize textual difficulties through a bifurcation. In Bixler's case, however, the chief division is not made externally, in James's works, but internally, in his temperament. Bixler wants to minimize contradiction in James by showing that his thought can be divided in accordance with his needs for both moralism and religion. Thus, according to Bixler, one part of James's work supports his impulse toward meaningful action, while the other part supports his need for intimacy.

Like the first explanatory theories I mentioned, these last four are also helpful. Suckiel's method of interpretation helps us avoid the indolence to which we might be led if we simply accept contradictions as typical in James's work. By looking deeper, past the rhetorical surfaces, we may find unexpected and insightful explanations. Although we may not expect all of the contradictions in James's work to be so neatly resolvable, Seigfried and Cooper's views take us further in the direction Suckiel indicates. Seigfried's view offers us a developmental model for ordering James's evolving thought. Cooper's view gives us two general contexts within which to interpret James's corpus. It warns us against the mistake of failing to take into account the definite scientific constraints that guide the writing of *Principles* or of trying to interpret *A Pluralistic Universe* in accordance with these constraints. Apart from the paradox of finding unity in James's thought by hypothesizing a "Two-Levels View," however, Cooper seems to want to separate the philosopher from the philosophy in a way that Bixler does not.[10] Bixler's procedure of distinguishing between the two sides of James's temperament and tracing out how these competing moods are expressed in his work seems more in keeping with the kind of analysis James himself might have made. Yet Bixler's interpretation is also problematic, since it leaves us without a way of bridging the gap between the two facets of James's temperament.

For Richard Gale, this inability to bridge the gap in James's temperament simply follows from an accurate understanding of James's life and thought. Gale presents his views in his book *The Divided Self of William James*, to which I would now like to turn in some detail. An examination of Gale's thesis will point out what I hold to be a some-what common mistake among interpreters of James—a mistake for which my Integration Thesis will serve as a corrective.

Gale gives us an impressively thorough and detailed analysis of many of the themes that lie at the heart of James's life and work. He takes James quite seriously and works out these themes with great care and rigor—a method that puts him in Seigfried's second camp of commentators. Just as impressive is Gale's ability to apply his rigorous method in a very playful and witty style. The result is an important and quite entertaining contribution to James scholarship.

Valuable as the book is, however, I believe there are problems with its basic thesis. Gale identifies two personas in James: a Promethean pragmatist and an anti-Promethean mystic. He argues that these personas clash, resulting in an unresolved and unresolvable tension. According to Gale, this clash results in a number of aporias James was never able to work through, so that the division in James's psyche is deep and synchronic. James is left with no other recourse than to spend his life singing "The Divided Self Blues." This basic thesis of Gale's book I propose to call the "Divided Self Thesis."

I believe the Divided Self Thesis represents a profound and pernicious misreading of James. I base this assessment on three different objections. My first objection is that, although James had mystical leanings (what he called a "germ" of mysticism) and although he had a deep respect for mystical experiences, he himself was not a mystical absolutist. My second objection is that the unresolvability of the clash Gale sees in James's temperament is due, in part, to the intellectualistic way Gale presents the problem. If, in a Jamesian spirit, we treat the problem concretely, much of the contradiction melts away. My third objection is that Gale does not consider powerful textual evidence that indicates real progress James made toward integrating these two parts of his psyche. I believe this textual evidence supports an Integration Thesis, my alternative to Gale's Divided Self Thesis. In the remainder of this chapter, I will explain more fully my first two objections to Gale's thesis, saving the third for the next chapter. But first, let us take a closer look at Gale's thesis itself.

GALE'S DIVIDED SELF THESIS

For Gale, James's two selves have such fundamentally different orientations to the world that they create a number of unresolvable aporias. As a Promethean pragmatist, for example, James values concepts instrumentally, seeing them as necessary tools for attaining what he desires. As an anti-Promethean mystic, on the other hand, James dispenses with concepts in favor of experiences of unification. Concepts are external interpretations that get in the way of the intimacy of immediate experience.

James's Promethean ethical theory, according to Gale, is based on the normative principle that "We are always morally obligated to act so as to maximize desire-satisfaction over desire-dissatisfaction."[11] James's mystical ethical theory, on the other hand, is more deontological, with normative claims not relativized to claims based on particular desires.

At the root of the clash between these two selves, Gale argues, is James's ambivalent attitude toward evil. As a Promethean, James wants a world of risk. As Gale puts it, "When James was in his healthy Promethean frame of mind he tingled all over at the thought that we are engaged in a Texas Death Match with evil, without any assurance of eventual victory, only the possibility of victory."[12] The tingling comes precisely from the as-yet-undecided status of the world in its struggle with evil. That evil will ultimately triumph is a real possibility. There is an energizing and exciting suspense that comes from this possibility, as when one is reading a mystery novel and resists the temptation to "cheat" by reading the last few pages first. But there is an added sense of meaning when the reader realizes she herself is the author. It is not simply that the outcome has not yet been discovered, but that the outcome has not yet been decided. But this indeterminateness, which is energizing in some moods, is terrifying in others. In these other moods, it is not a moral challenge James seeks, but intimacy and comfort. Gale writes, "In order to 'help him make it through the night,' [James] needs a mystically based religion, which gives him a sense of absolute safety and peace that comes through union with an encompassing spiritual reality."[13] At these times, Gale argues, James needs the assurance that evil is illusory, or at least that it will surely be defeated.

Gale's Promethean James emphasizes the future in his theory of meaning, identifying a concept with a set of conditionalized predictions, whereas his mystical James emphasizes the present, interpreting mystical claims by the content of mystical experiences.

For the Promethean James, God is a concept that helps us access our deepest powers in our fight against evil.[14] For the mystical James, on the other hand, God can best be understood in the context of experiences of a unifying presence.

Gale calls the most important clash between James's Promethean and mystical selves the "Big Aporia." This is the clash between Promethean "Ontological Relativism" and mystical absolutism. Gale defines Ontological Relativism as the view that "all reality claims must be relativized to a person at a time." Mysticism, on the other hand, makes "absolute, nonrelativized reality claims . . . based on mystical experiences."[15]

Gale develops his Divided Self Thesis in impressive detail. Starting with James's Promethean ethics, he moves through discussions of belief, will, freedom, and truth. In the second part of his book, he contrasts these views with James's mystical quest for unity. There is much to be said for and about Gale's close reading and insightful interpretations of James's texts. As for Gale's overall thesis about James, however, I believe it to be fundamentally mistaken.

I do agree with Gale's identification of the primary tension in James's life and work as the clash between the Promethean and the mystic. As we have already seen, Bixler makes a similar identification in his *Religion in the Philosophy of William James*, published in 1926. Bixler, whose work Gale does not reference, identifies the tension in James's thought as arising largely out of a personal struggle between the active and the passive approaches to life. Bixler writes:

> James seems to have found two souls within his breast. . . . On the one hand he felt the press of the active impulses, their aggressive demands for power, their challenge to the environment and their eager desire to remake it. . . . But on the other hand he was not insensitive to the more passive desire for assurance, stability, and comfort. In the one mood James is ready to scale the highest heaven in his quest for value or to penetrate the deepest abyss in his insistence on the triumphantly conquering and creative ability of the human spirit. In the other his whole being longs for peace. . . .[16]

While Gale identifies this division in James to be a synchronic one that leaves James singing "The Divided Self Blues" to the end of his life, Bixler argues that James actually chose decisively in favor of his active, pluralistic soul. I believe Gale and Bixler are both wrong; there is strong textual evidence that James chose *both* the pragmatic *and* the mystical in an attempt to integrate the two. While Bixler acknowledges some of James's progress in this regard, Gale does not. In the next chapter, we will examine the textual evidence supporting my position. In the remainder of this chapter, we will consider two other very significant difficulties with Gale's account.

OBJECTIONS TO GALE'S ACCOUNT OF JAMES

The first objection concerns Gale's mystical reading of James. Gale claims, ". . . the mystical aspects of James's texts that I shall bring to light are far more prevalent and important than any expositor has realized, and . . . any acceptable interpretation must provide an important place for them."[17] Had Gale known of Bixler's work, he no doubt would have had some sympathy with it. Bixler has an entire chapter on James's mysticism. His sympathetic account of this mysticism might help Gale see that, although James's mystical sympathies do form a very important part of his work that some readers would rather ignore than acknowledge, Gale's James is more mystical than text and biography indicate the historical James to have been.

In taking up James's relation to mysticism, Gale notes James's well-known claims not to have had any mystical experiences:

> Surprisingly, James claims not to have had any mystical experiences himself—"my own consitution shuts me out from their enjoyment almost entirely, and I can speak of them only at second hand" (VRE 301). If this is so, is not the underlying thesis of this book, that James had a mystical self that clashed with his Promethean pragmatic self, especially in regard to the challenges posed by evil, wrong? How can one be a mystic, or even be so sympathetically inclined to mystical experiences as to accept their cognitivity, as James will be seen to have done, without having mystical experiences?[18]

Gale devotes less than two out of the more than 350 pages in his book to answering these very important questions—far too little space in my view to address them adequately. He gives two answers. First, he argues that one need not be a mystic to appreciate mystical experience, any more than one need be Beethoven to resonate aesthetically to the *Eroica* Symphony. Second, he claims that James was

> not leveling with his audience. Mystical experiences for him cover a broad spectrum of cases, ranging from the relatively undeveloped experiences of a heightened sense of reality, an intensification of feeling and insight such as occurs under the influence of alcohol, drugs, nitrous oxide, art, and even the raptures of nature, to the fully developed monistic experience of an undifferentiated unity in which all distinctions are obliterated. James never had an experience of the latter kind, but he did have more than his share of the less developed ones. . . .[19]

I think Gale's answers are accurate, but inadequate to support his mystical portrait of James. First, it is clear that one need not be a composer to resonate aesthetically to beautiful music, but it is just as clear that a listener will not resonate to the music *in the same way* as its composer. Second, if it is true, as indeed I think it is, that James never had a "fully developed monistic experience of an undifferentiated unity in which all distinctions are obliterated," then it is important not to ascribe to him positions he merely defends as legitimate for those who *have* had them. While I agree with Gale that James had more in the way of mystical experiences than he let on, I also think it is important not to lose sight of the relatively moderate, non-absolutist level of James's mystical experience. Gale concludes his short examination of this objection, ". . . James had every right to be a sympathetic expositor and defender of mysticism."[20] This is quite true, but it does not make James himself a *full-fledged* mystic. Gale's Big Aporia that we discussed earlier involves a clash between a Promethean Ontological Relativism that relativizes all reality claims to a person at a time and a mystical absolutism that bases reality claims on mystical experiences that render them nonrelativized. Gale seems to hold that all cases of mysticism are cases of mystical absolutism. An alternative view is that mystical absolutism holds only for cases of fully developed mysticism. That James espouses this second view seems evident when he writes, "Mystical states, *when well developed*, usually are, and have the right to be absolutely authoritative over the individuals to whom they come. . . . As a matter of psychological fact, mystical states *of a well-pronounced and emphatic sort* are usually authoritative over those who have them" (VRE, 335, italics added). Full-fledged mystics, as a rule, do not try to relativize the absolute claims that arise from their experience. So Gale's Big Aporia is rarely, if ever, an issue for them. And if it is true, as I contend, that mystical absolutism is not a feature of the level of mysticism James experienced, then the Big Aporia is not an issue for James either—even when he relativizes his mystical experiences. I conclude that Gale's Big Aporia is not as troublesome as he makes it out to be, since it is only those (like James) whose mysticism is not absolute who typically are tempted to relativize its reality claims.

This, in brief, is my first objection to Gale's reading of James. But even if the Big Aporia does not apply to James, he still faces the task of integrating his lower-level mysticism with his pragmatism. My second and third objections to Gale's Thesis concern this remaining task. [21]

My second objection is that Gale's account involves an intellectualization of the division in James's psyche. Gale separates from each other two parts of James's experience, names them, and describes them in great detail. Then he shows how they cannot be reconciled. But this whole process is one example of the intellectualization James so decried. There *is* a real problem here, but it cuts deeper than the conflict between these two straw men. The Promethean pragmatist is supposed to be interested in nothing that cannot be used for some end. But this pragmatist is supposed to be so narrow-minded that he cannot see that one of the things he wants is experiences of a mystical sort, experiences that cannot directly be used for something else, experiences that he values for themselves. The mystic, on the other hand, is portrayed as someone who has given up all use of the will and is merely a passive receiver of rich experience. Downplayed here is the *practice* of mysticism. For most mystics, it takes a lot of difficult, volitional labor to come to the point of giving up the will in the richness of experience. And for many mystics, their religious experience is a catalyst for volitional labor to be taken up once the experience is over. As James writes in *Varieties* of his distinctions between the healthy and the morbid mind and between the once-born and the twice-born types, the distinction between pragmatism and mysticism ceases to be the radical antagonism which many think it to be (VRE, 385n). Pragmatists do depend, to a greater or lesser degree, on mystical experiences of some sort; and mystics do depend, to a greater or lesser degree, on a pragmatic approach to life. No one of us can be purely active or purely passive in life. So the real question is not which we will choose, but how we will integrate the two. The challenge of integration may not be so great in a person for whom one or the other pole is very pronounced. But when an individual, like James, deeply values both pragmatism and mysticism, the challenge of integration is likely to be especially great.

Gale offers James a choice: be a pragmatist or be a mystic. It is impossible, he argues, to choose both. This begins to sound a lot like a certain dilemma in philosophy that served as a point of departure for James. In the first of his *Pragmatism* lectures, James identifies the then-current choice in philosophy as one between rationalism and empiricism, between religious and scientific philosophies. Arguing that philosophy is a function of temperament, he claims that individuals of a tender-minded temperament will opt for the rationalistic, religious choice, while those of a tough-minded temperament will go for the empiricist, scientific choice. But James observes that few of us are radically tender-minded or radically tough-minded; instead, most of us are a mixture of the two. He predicts that many of us will be dissatisfied with the limited range of options, since neither is in keeping with our temperament. To remedy the situation, he offers pragmatism as an alternative, expecting it to have a broader appeal, since it corresponds to a mixed temperament of the sort most of us have.

The present situation is quite similar. Gale presents us with a choice between Promethean pragmatism and anti-Promethean mysticism. Yet few of us—and this holds true for James, as well—are of a radically Promethean or of a radically anti-Promethean temperament. Like James, we have a need for both freedom and intimacy. We need both space and place—space in which to act and place in which to find comfort and security. What we long for is a way to integrate these two ways of living life. But integration does not mean reduction to homogeneity like the integration of the hot and the cold results in the banality of the tepid. We want, like Jonathan Edwards, to live our lives with all our might, but we do not want to be forced to an unbalanced extremism to do it.

The tension in James between the need for the challenge of freedom and the need for the reassurance of intimacy is palpable. Pointing out ways in which James worked to resolve this tension is valuable for James scholarship. It may prove to be of value, as well, in the lives of those of his readers who experience a similar tension and are looking for concrete, practical ways of diminishing it.

Seen not as an intellectualistic puzzle, but in this deeper, more concrete way, we can find cause for hope in James's texts. *Pace* Gale's synchronic account of a James singing "The Divided Self Blues" to his dying day, I believe James actually made real progress toward integrating his two selves. This is my Integration Thesis. According to this thesis, James made significant progress in integrating his pragmatic and mystical sides in the last ten years of his life. Noticeable in *Varieties* and in *Pragmatism*, this progress is especially pronounced in *A Pluralistic Universe* and in *Some Problems of Philosophy*. In the next chapter, we will turn to some of the strong textual evidence that supports the Integration Thesis. Before we do so, however, let us explore a common mistake to which interpreters of James are susceptible. An understanding of this mistake will help clarify what I mean by the Integration Thesis and why I embrace it.

SNIPPING THE REFLEX ARC

James's career at Harvard began with his teaching of physiology in 1873. He soon moved to teaching psychology and eventually philosophy, but although he stopped teaching physiology, he by no means left it behind. One of the most important influences of physiology on James's later thought can be seen in his use of the reflex action theory, a theory we examined in some detail in chapter 2. In "Reflex Action and Theism," James calls the reflex action theory a "fundamental and well established" physiological model. He points out that this theory "dominates all the new work done in psychology," and calls it a "great achievement of our generation" (WB, 93). We have already seen how heavily James's own psychology is influenced by the reflex action theory. James's philosophical works, too—including *The Will to Believe*, *The Varieties of Religious Experience*, *Pragmatism*, *A Pluralistic Universe*, and *Some Problems of Philosophy*, presuppose and make at least oblique reference to this physiological model. If James's thought has an identifiable center of vision, the reflex action theory must certainly be a part of it.

According to the reflex action theory, as we have seen, the nervous system is composed of three interrelated elements: sensory nerves (Department One), nerve centers (Department Two), and motor nerves (Department Three). The reflex arc is understood as a dynamic system, with nerve currents flowing in, being processed, and then flowing out again. Any disruption to this dynamism is indicative of malfunction. And yet a common temptation among James interpreters is to try to snip the reflex arc. Some try to excise a part of the reflex arc; others leave all the parts in place, but attempt to sever their connections. Among the first group of commentators is Ellen Suckiel, who in effect snips the reflex arc when she identifies James's methodological commitment to the principle of experience and his teleological conception of human nature to be the two pillars of James's pragmatism.[22] She stresses experience (Department One) and teleology (Department Three), but snips out the bottom of the reflex arc loop by leaving out conception (Department Two). (Note, as well, that there is no dynamism in the notion of a philosophical view grounded on two *pillars*.)

Bixler wants to snip the reflex arc in a similar way. In identifying religion and moralism as the two poles that define James's thought, he leaves conception out of account. Religion, emphasizing the passive receptivity of experience, belongs chiefly to perception; and moralism, emphasizing active interests, belongs chiefly to volition. Thus, Bixler snips out the middle part of the loop and leaves Department One and Department Three in static, oppositional relation. Now James must struggle between the two and finally make his decision for one or the other.

Gale, too, wants to snip the reflex arc, but instead of excising Department Two, he simply wants to sever connections between Department One and Departments Two and Three. Unlike Suckiel and Bixler, Gale emphasizes the instrumental importance of concepts for James—or at least for James's Promethean self. Instead of excising the conceptual part of the reflex arc loop entirely, he wants to make a cut between Departments One and Two. On the one side is left the mystical self, which emphasizes the attempt to find intimacy and unity by jettisoning concepts, and on the other is the volitional, Promethean self with its empowering conception of the world.

Gale has responded to this critique by claiming that, according to James, the reflex arc is normatively, but not factually, fundamental to experience, and that the reflex arc holds for only part of experience.[23] Gale contends that there is much to be said for the position that action should follow sensation and conception, but that this occurs only in the context of Promethean pragmatism. He argues that James himself held mystical experiences to constitute a class of exceptions to the reflex arc, and he offers two arguments to support what he claims was James's position. First, he argues that mystical experiences do not result in the kinds of actions predicted by the reflex arc. Of the motor effects that result from the reflex arc, Gale writes, "Supposedly the resulting actions are *motor actions* consisting in the movement of limbs, not just any physical changes within the subject that are the effects of the processing in the nerve centers."[24] On this basis, Gale argues that mystical experiences do not conform to the reflex arc type, since these experiences do not lead to specific motor actions. Second, Gale argues that mystical experiences are absolutely ineffable (i.e., nonconceptualizable), so they cannot be conceptualized in the second department of the reflex arc.

A careful reading of James's work shows Gale's claims regarding the reflex arc to be inaccurate. They are based on an unfortunate misunderstanding of James's views on the reflex action theory and of the pervasive use he makes of them in his thinking and writing. James, in fact, does not acknowledge mystical experiences as constituting exceptions to the reflex action model. Gerald E. Myers writes, "James thought the evidence shows that reflex action or the direct production of movement upon the presence of a sensible impression operates throughout the whole of consciousness, so that every sensation, feeling, or idea tends to discharge in some motor or movement effect."[25] One of Gale's mistakes is to suppose that the discharge James has in mind must be a motor action. In a number of different passages, James is quite careful to separate himself from this view. In *The Principles of Psychology*, for example, James writes:

> That [mental phenomena] lead to *acts* is of course the most familiar of truths, but I do not merely mean acts in the sense of voluntary and deliberate muscular performances. Mental states occasion also changes in the caliber of blood-vessels, or alteration in the

heart-beats, or processes more subtle still, in glands and viscera. If these are taken into account, as well as acts which follow at some *remote period* because the mental state was once there, it will be safe to lay down the general law that *no mental modification ever occurs which is not accompanied or followed by a bodily change.* (PP, 18)

Again, in *Talks to Teachers*, James writes:

The fact is that there is no sort of consciousness whatever, be it sensation, feeling, or idea, which does not directly and of itself tend to discharge into some motor effect. The motor effect need not always be an outward stroke of behavior. It may be only an alteration of the heart-beats or breathing, or a modification in the distribution of blood, such as blushing or turning pale; or else a secretion of tears, or what not. But in any case, it is there in some shape when any consciousness is there; and a belief as fundamental as any in modern psychology is the belief at last attained that conscious processes of any sort, conscious processes merely as such, *must* pass over into motion, open or concealed. (TT, 102)

Turning now from general statements about all of experience to a specific claim about mysticism, we find that James writes in *Varieties*: "Mystical states, strictly so called, are never merely interruptive. Some memory of their content always remains, and a profound sense of their importance. They modify the inner life of the subject between the times of their recurrence" (VRE, 303).

So much then for Gale's claim that mystical states do not follow the reflex arc because they do not lead to action. What about his claim that mystical states do not follow the reflex arc because they are absolutely ineffable and thus nonconceptualizable? I would say, once again, that this is another example of Gale's intellectualism at play. Because mystical states are characterized as ineffable, not only can we not say anything about them, but we cannot even conceptualize them. Although it is not possible to do complete justice to mystical states when we speak or think about them, speak and think about them we clearly do. No experience, for James, is fully accessible to words and concepts. But that does not mean they can capture nothing of the reality we use them to describe. Mystical experience is particularly difficult to speak and think about, but that does not mean that nothing we say or think about it has any merit whatsoever. But even if Gale were right that mystical states are absolutely ineffable and nonconceptualizable, this would simply mean that they exist in what James, referring implicitly to the reflex arc, describes in *Varieties* as the "short circuit" between feeling and conduct that bypasses theories, ideas, and symbols.

If mystical states do not constitute an exception to the reflex arc, are there other types of experiences that do? Gale thinks there are and adduces an example from James to try to show that other types of sensations do not terminate in overt actions. He quotes James as follows:

> The habit of excessive novel-reading and theatre-going will produce true monsters in the line. The weeping of a Russian lady over the fictitious personages in the play, while her coachman is freezing to death on his seat outside, is the sort of thing that everywhere happens on a less glaring scale. . . . One becomes filled with emotions which habitually pass without prompting to any deed, and so the inertly sentimental condition is kept up. The remedy would be, never to suffer one's self to have an emotion . . . without expressing it afterwards in *some* active way. (PP, 129–30)

Gale concludes from this that action in this case would be laudable, but that it is by no means necessary. Thus, Gale thinks this provides a counterexample to the reflex action theory. But Gale simply misses James's point here. Just before citing the example Gale quotes, James writes, "Every time a resolve or a fine glow of feeling evaporates without bearing practical fruit is worse than a chance lost; it works so as positively to hinder future resolutions and emotions from taking the normal path of discharge." It is not that there is no effect in cases such as these, but that the effect is a bad one. In the paragraph immediately following the one from which Gale quotes, James refers to the case of the Russian lady and similar ones as follows:

> These latter cases make us more aware that it is not simply *particular lines* of discharge, but also *general forms* of discharge, that seem to be grooved out by habit in the brain. Just as, if we let our emotions evaporate, they get into a way of evaporating; so there is reason to suppose that if we often flinch from making an effort, before we know it the effort-making capacity will be gone; and that, if we suffer the wandering of our attention, presently it will wander all the time. (PP, 130)

Thus, James's point with the example Gale cites is not that the Russian lady's reflex arc should have led to some form of discharge, but did not. Rather, James's point clearly is that it led to a discharge (since it could not do otherwise), but that this discharge reinforced a bad habit. "The inertly sentimental condition is kept up." So *pace* Gale, James holds that the reflex arc is both factually and normatively fundamental for experience. Factually, all sensations and thoughts eventually lead to some type of motion; normatively, we have at least some control over the types of motion to which they will lead, and we should exercise this control in favor of discharges that will be good for ourselves and others.[26] In addition, James holds that the reflex arc is fundamental to all types of conscious experience, not excepting mystical and emotional ones.

In conclusion, no account of James that leaves out the organic dynamism of the reflex arc can be accurate. As a physiological model, the reflex arc involves incoming nerve currents that cannot simply stop; they must be discharged somehow. James is consistent throughout his life and work in arguing for this dynamism. Where he is not consistent is in identifying the part of the dynamism he values most. In his early work, including *The Will to Believe*, he claims that volition is the most important part of the reflex arc. In *The Varieties of Religious Experience*, he emphasizes perception and downplays the role of volition. The central claim of my Integration Thesis, to which we will now turn, addresses this inconsistency.

CHAPTER 5

The Integration Thesis

The Integration Thesis holds that, beginning with *Varieties*, but most noticeably in *A Pluralistic Universe* and *Some Problems of Philosophy*, James begins to integrate various dimensions of his thought. This integration is most noticeable in the religious dimension,[1] where it can be characterized as a process of unification or a gradual conversion of a heterogeneous personality. Many have speculated as to how James should be classed in accordance with the categories he sets up in *Varieties*. The usual speculation centers around James's appropriation of Renouvier, which ended the depression of his late twenties. I do not intend to minimize the importance of that experience for James or to deny its value for understanding *Varieties* and James's own personal experiential position relative to it. However, I want to focus on another conversion that occurred in the last ten years of James's life.

James's second conversion is a gradual one, in which he makes progress toward the reconciliation of various conflicting parts of his thought. He speaks directly of one event in this process as an "inner catastrophe," and doubts that his words will be able to "convert" his audience to a similar point of view (PU, 118, 131–2). The specifically religious ramification of this conversion is James's articulation of a position he once thought impossible—namely, that of the overcoming of the radical discord between moralism and religion (ERM, 62–3). In the psychological dimension, the integration takes place principally between perception and conception, although there is also some evidence for integration between perception and volition, as well. It would be a mistake to expect James's integration to be carried out as completely in the psychological dimension as it is in the religious, since James's attention has largely turned from psychology to metaphysics before the conversion begins. In the sociological realm, the integration is reflected in James's balanced description of the university as an institution capable of an important social contribution.

MINIMIZING UNNECESSARY TENSION

The Integration Thesis does not imply that all tension can—or should—be eliminated from James's thought. Given his view of the failure of conceptualization, it would be problematic to claim the conceptual integration in any area of his thought to be complete. The Integration Thesis is simply a way of minimizing unnecessary tension in James's corpus.

With this sketch of the Integration Thesis in mind, let us now consider in greater detail some of the effects of James's conversion on his thinking. It will be important not only to discuss the effects James works out explicitly but also to develop what James's views might have looked like had he worked out the changes in all dimensions of his thought.

Metaphysics

The first indication of integration in the religious realm occurs with James's discussion of healthy-minded religion in *Varieties*. As we saw in chapter 3, James writes, in the introduction to *Literary Remains*, of a radical discord between moralism and religion. In this work, published in 1884, James distinguishes between the healthy-minded and the morbid view of life. But he consistently identifies healthy-mindedness with moralism and morbid-mindedness with religion. Perhaps this radical bifurcation is one he has inherited from his father, who, according to James, "pitted religion and [moralism] against each other as enemies of whom one must die utterly, if the other is to live in genuine form." James goes on to state his own opinion that the "accord of moralism and religion is superficial, their discord radical. Only the deepest thinkers on both sides see that one must go" (ERM, 62–3). Some fifteen years later, in *Varieties*, James does not find such a radical discord between healthy-minded moralism and morbid-minded religion. When James writes of a "healthy-minded religion" in the later work, he is advocating the legitimacy of a middle position between the disjuncts of his earlier bifurcation.

James's initial move toward integration in *Varieties* is an important indication of what is to come. He continues his project of integration to a much greater extent in *A Pluralistic Universe*, where he details his own religious over-beliefs. As we have seen, James there examines the Gods of theism, idealism, and radical empiricism. This examination is in accordance with what he defends as his right to decide genuine options in religion on the basis of his passional interests. His rejection of the first two Gods in favor of the last can best be understood in terms of his project of integration. James is looking for a God who can satisfy the needs of both moralism and religion. That is, he is looking for a God who can provide both maximum meaning and maximum intimacy. Both needs are threatened if God is either too big or too small. For our place in the universe to be meaningful, God must be small enough to leave us room for meaningful contributions, yet big enough to guarantee the survival of our moral selves after our biological selves have died. For us to be able to have an intimate relationship with God, he must be small enough to be like us, yet big enough to provide us with help and comfort when we feel weak.

Given these requirements, it is no wonder that James is not satisfied with the traditional theistic God. The problem with such a God is that he is simply too big. In accordance with James's view, theism's claim that both God and truth are complete and independent of us leaves us with no ultimately meaningful purpose. Metaphysically, all is decided, and nothing is left for us to do but to work to establish the ethical will of God on earth as it is metaphysically established in heaven. Our highest role is only that of obedient servants, a role that is not meaningful enough to satisfy James.

Just as the theistic God is too big to allow for the meaning James seeks, he is also too big to satisfy James's need for intimacy. Because he is independent of us, he cannot be affected by our prayers or moved by our pleas for aid. Thus, he is simply too big to provide us with help and comfort when we need it.[2]

The idealistic God, the Absolute, has some advantages over the theistic God. The notion that we are entitatively one with the Absolute, for example, overcomes the theistic rift between creature and creator. Despite its advantages, however, the Absolute is also too big to meet the needs for meaning and intimacy. If reality is defined by the point of view of the Absolute, according to which all is well with the universe, it is hard to see how any human action can have ultimate significance. Furthermore, it is hard to feel intimacy with the Absolute, since it is so wholly other from us. James calls the Absolute a "metaphysical monster" and points out that it "neither acts nor suffers, nor loves nor hates; it has no needs, desires, or aspirations, no failures or successes, friends or enemies, victories or defeats" (PU, 26, 27). How can we feel safe and secure in the knowledge that all is well with the Absolute, James asks, if it is so foreign to us and if its wellness in no way translates into positive practical results in our world? The Absolute's existence is apparently compatible with all sorts of evil in its respective parts and does not allow us to hope for the triumph of any particular good over any particular evil.

Although James argues that the "outlines of the superhuman consciousness ... must remain ... very vague" (PU, 140), these outlines are detailed enough to show that the God of radical empiricism fares better than either the theistic God or the idealistic Absolute in maximizing both meaning and intimacy. James's God is both small enough and large enough to render human action meaningful. He[3] is small enough, since evil lies outside of him and forms an enemy we can join him in fighting. Victory over evil is not assured, as it is on the other two metaphysical hypotheses. Our individual efforts in this fight may provide the critical moral energy necessary to defeat the enemy. This is all the more probable since we are constitutive elements of God's consciousness. The God of radical empiricism is also large enough that these individual efforts of ours will not merely disappear at our biological death. Since God's mind is composed, at least in part, of our individual selves, and since God survives the death of those individual selves, he guarantees our moral survival. That is, he guarantees that our biological death will not end the effects of our individual contributions in the moral struggle.

James's God is also both small enough and large enough to have intimate relationships with human beings. Both the theistic God and the idealistic Absolute seem incapable of identifying with the interests of individuals. Their thoughts are not our thoughts, nor are their ways our ways. What intimacy can we have with Gods who are infinite in their perfections? James's God, on the other hand, is finite. Because of this finitude and because we are actually constitutive elements in God's consciousness, we can rest assured that God is like us and that we are like him. James writes, "Having an environment, being in time, and working out a history just like ourselves, he escapes from the foreignness from all that is human ... " (PU, 144). God is larger than we are, however, and still remains powerful enough to give us comfort when we need it. Although God is dependent on each of us, we are not the only individuals on whom he depends. This makes it possible for us to take what James calls a "moral holiday" from time to time. We can take an occasional break from the moral struggle in order to relax and find comfort and reassurance that God's is the winning side.

At this point, the nature of the integration of James's religious views should be clear. What he had initially seen, in *Literary Remains*, as radically bifurcated, he tries to integrate in two stages. In *Varieties*, he carries out the integration at the level of religious experience by introducing a healthy-minded religion; in *A Pluralistic Universe*, he works out the integration further by developing a theology for a God who is compatible with such an integration.[4]

Psychology

In addition to this metaphysical integration, James also works toward an epistemological integration of his views. It will be appropriate to discuss this second integration in psychological terms since it involves the integration of the psychological faculties of perception, conception, and volition.

Perception and Conception

It may initially seem hopelessly difficult to make a case for the integration of perception and conception in James's thought. After all, James contends throughout his work that conception is a secondary faculty. We have already noted his claim in "Reflex Action and Theism" that conception (as well as perception) is secondary to volition. He states, "The willing department of our nature . . . dominates both the conceiving department and the feeling department; or, in plainer English, perception and thinking are only there for behavior's sake" (WB, 92). We have also seen that, in *Varieties*, James contrasts reason with perception and volition and not only claims that reason is less important for religion than the other two parts of the self, but even goes so far as to say that reason is not always necessary for religion. In a passage we examined in chapter 3, he writes:

> The theories which Religion generates, being thus variable, are secondary; and if you wish to grasp her essence, you must look to the feelings and the conduct as being the more constant elements. It is between these two elements that the short circuit exists on which she carries on her principal business, while the ideas and symbols and other institutions form loop-lines which may be perfections and improvements, and may even some day all be united into one harmonious system, but which are not to be regarded as organs with an indispensable function, necessary at all times for religious life to go on. (VRE, 397)

In *Some Problems of Philosophy*, he writes, "Conception is a secondary process, not indispensable to life. It presupposes perception, which is self-sufficing . . . " (SPP, 46).

Despite these passages, I believe James moves toward an integrated view of perception and conception. To show why I believe this, I want to consider carefully the two main senses in which the term "secondary" is used and to show what effect these senses have on our understanding of the claim that conception is secondary to perception. In the first sense, the term "secondary" is used temporally to indicate that one event happens subsequently to another. It is in this sense that an effect is said to be secondary to its cause. In accordance with this meaning, the claim in question is that conception is *temporally secondary* to perception. This claim is part of the empiricist position that nothing is in the mind except what was first in the senses. Given James's empiricism, it is no surprise that he holds this empiricist tenet.[5]

There is, however, a second sense in which the term can be used. In this sense, "secondary" indicates that one thing is less important than another. Thus, a secondary road is less important than an interstate highway. In accordance with this definition, the claim in question is that conception is *secondary in importance* to perception. This claim goes beyond empiricism to anti-intellectualism. If intellectualism holds that percepts are secondary in importance to concepts, anti-intellectualism, in opposing this view, can be described as having a weaker and a stronger form. Weak anti-intellectualism claims that neither percepts nor concepts are secondary in importance to each other. That is, percepts and concepts are equally important to the individual. Strong anti-intellectualism claims that concepts are secondary in importance to percepts. Although the passages I quoted at the beginning of this section seem to portray James as a strong anti-intellectualist, my contention is that he moves toward weak anti-intellectualism, which is in accordance with an integrated view of the self. In support of this contention, I will first document the weak anti-intellectualism that enters James's writings in the last few years of his life and then indicate how this renders problematic any application of strong anti-intellectualism to the human self.

I have already quoted passages in which James describes the intellect as secondary in importance to perception. In these passages, he even goes so far as to claim that the intellect is inessential for life and for at least some forms of religion. This strong anti-intellectualism is contrasted with descriptions of a very different sort that appear in his later works. In *Pragmatism*, for example, he supports the weak anti-intellectualistic claim that both concepts and percepts are necessary for life. He writes:

> We are like fishes swimming in the sea of sense, bounded above
> by the superior element, but unable to breathe it pure or penetrate
> it. We get our oxygen from it, however, we touch it incessantly,
> now in this part, now in that, and every time we touch it, we turn
> back into the water with our course re-determined and re-
> energized. The abstract ideas of which the air consists are indis-
> pensable for life, but irrespirable by themselves, as it were, and
> only active in their re-directing function. (P, 64)

In *A Pluralistic Universe*, James praises the human capacity for
conceptualization. "Both theoretically and practically," he writes, "this
power of framing abstract concepts is one of the sublimest of our
human prerogatives" (PU, 98–9). Nowhere does James state more clearly
the equally important functions of perception and conception than in
Some Problems of Philosophy. He there claims, "Percepts and concepts
interpenetrate and melt together, impregnate and fertilize each other.
Neither, taken alone, knows reality in its completeness. We need them
both, as we need both our legs to walk with" (SPP, 34). In another
passage in the same book, writing again of percepts and concepts, he
states: "For some purposes the one, for other purposes the other, has
the higher value. Who can decide offhand which is absolutely better
to live or to understand life? We must do both alternately, and a man
can no more limit himself to either than a pair of scissors can cut with
a single one of its blades" (SPP, 43–4).

	Thus, on the one hand, James claims, "Conception is a secondary
process, not indispensable to life. It presupposes perception, which is
self-sufficing." And on the other hand, he claims that "abstract
ideas . . . are indispensable to life" and that "both [universal and particular parts of experience] are indispensable." This apparent contradiction can be resolved by making a distinction between the kind of
life for which conception is "indispensable" and the kind of life for
which it is "not indispensable." There is good textual evidence that
James believes that conception is not indispensable for animal life in
general, but that it is indispensable for normal human life.

	In *A Pluralistic Universe*, James claims that the ability to concep-
tualize is the main advantage human beings have over animals (PU,
98).[6] In a later passage in the same book, James states that animals live
exclusively—and narrowly—in "sensible reality" (PU, 110). Similarly,
in *Some Problems of Philosophy*, James writes, "Sensation and thought in
man are mingled. . . . In our quadrupedal relatives thought proper is
at a minimum . . . " (SPP, 31). In the same book, he adduces "all lower
creatures in whom conscious life goes on by reflex adaptations" to
show that perception is self-sufficing (SPP, 46). If taken by itself, then,

self-sufficing perception yields experience of the sort that *animals* have, and it is correct to conclude that conception is not indispensable to life of this sort.[7] But in *human* life, perception and conception are mingled. Later in *Some Problems of Philosophy*, James explains more clearly what he means by this mingling:

> The universal and the particular parts of the experience are liter-ally immersed in each other, and both are indispensable. . . . Per-ception awakens thought, and thought in turn enriches perception. The more we see, the more we think; while the more we think, the more we see in our immediate experiences, and the greater grows the detail, and the more significant the articulateness of our per-ception. (SPP, 58, 59)[8]

I conclude that James's strong anti-intellectualism obtains only within the context of stating the conditions of possibility for the rudi-mentary life of animals and that only his weak anti-intellectualism applies to the full figure of the human self. For humans, concepts are, indeed, temporally secondary to percepts, but they are not secondary to them in importance.

Perception and Volition

In this context, perception means for James the passive receptivity of experience, whereas volition is the active choice of one among several possible responses to experience. As such, the question whether per-ception or volition is the essential element of the self is the psychologi-cal version of the religious option between passive and active religions. Because James's final response to the religious option is an integration of the two alternatives, it is only to be expected that his choice be-tween perception and volition will reflect a similar move toward inte-gration. Whether James actually carries this integration through on the psychological level is unclear from his writings. This is not too sur-prising, since by the time James arrives at the metaphysical integra-tion, he has stopped writing on psychology proper. What is clear from James's writings is the need for an integration of two contrary views, as well as a hint of James's openness to such an integration.

We have already noted James's statement in "Reflex Action and Theism" that identifies volition as the primary faculty of the self. Stress-ing the teleological nature of the self, he claims that both perception and conception are subservient to volition. We have also noted, by contrast, James's contention in *Varieties* that feeling is the basis of in-dividuality and noted the dislocation of volition in this work, which is due in part to James's elitism. How might the Integration Thesis help resolve this inconsistency?

A hint of the possibility of such a resolution can be found in James's definition of the "spiritual self" in *Principles*. He defines the self to be a person's inner or subjective being and claims that this subjective being has a central part that forms the "self of all the other selves." He describes it further as follows:

> Probably all men would describe it in much the same way up to a certain point. They would call it the *active* element in all consciousness; saying that whatever qualities a man's feelings may possess, or whatever content his thought may include, there is a spiritual something in him which seems to *go out* to meet these qualities and contents, whilst they seem to *come in* to be received by it. It is what welcomes or rejects. It presides over the perception of sensations, and by giving or withholding its assent it influences the movements they tend to arouse. It is the home of interest,—not the pleasant or the painful, not even pleasure or pain, as such, but that within us to which pleasure and pain, the pleasant and the painful, speak. It is the source of effort and attention, and the place from which appear to emanate the fiats of the will. . . . [It is] a sort of junction at which sensory ideas terminate and from which motor ideas proceed, and [forms] a kind of link between the two. (PP, 285)

At first blush, this passage seems to be in keeping with the volitional view of the self James has expressed in "Reflex Action and Theism." He writes that this essence of the self is the "active element in all consciousness," that it is the "home of interest," the "source of effort and attention, and the place from which appear to emanate the fiats of the will." But mixed in with all this activity there is also an undercurrent of passivity. The essence of the self is what *receives* the qualities and contents of perception; it is what "welcomes or rejects"; it is "that within us to which pleasure and pain, the pleasant and the painful, speak."

James gives two different pictures in this passage of the relation between this "self of selves" and the process of reflex adaptation. On the one hand, he describes the central part of the self as presiding over perception and as influencing the results it would normally trigger. On the other hand, this element of the self *is* the link between sensory ideas and motor ideas. If we understand this link in a Jamesian way, not as a point that would, in turn, require other mediational links to relate it to that which it links together, but as containing internally the relations between it and that which it links together, then we can begin to see how perception and volition are to be integrated.[9] If motor ideas are a part of volition, then the central self is the junction or nexus between perception and volition. It is the place, belonging exclusively neither to perception nor to volition, where the first is reflected or transformed into the second. Essential to this process is both the feeling that founds individuality, which is the focal point of *Varieties*, and the willing department that determines the teleology of the self, which is stressed in "Reflex Action and Theism." Without perception, the will would have nothing from which to choose; without volition, adaptations would be merely instinctual.

I will not insist too strongly that James ever consciously worked out such an integration between perception and volition. I will leave it as an observation that he *could* have and as a suggestion that he *may* have. What I *will* insist on, however, is that such an integration is needed.

Sociology

We have already noted that the tension in James's sociological writings on individualism is not as great as the tension in his psychological, and especially in his metaphysical writings. James bases his psychological and metaphysical writings on the reflex action model of the self, a model whose parts tend to get pulled out of balance, especially in his writings on religion. The closely related selection model, on which his sociological views are based, seems to be more stable. On this model, geniuses and non-geniuses, who are analogous to perception and conception on the reflex action model, are understood to be equally important for social progress. The stability of the selection model notwithstanding, we have seen that there is one important area of tension in James's sociology. In the first chapter, I pointed out James's early criticism of institutions, especially as evidenced by his attacks on the church. Since James sees institutions as social products of the intellect, it follows that this antagonism toward the church—along with his rebellion against the scientific community and his critique of the government—is a function of his anti-intellectualism. After his second conversion, when James softens his epistemological anti-intellectualism, he also modifies his anti-institutionalism and emphasizes important functions for institutions as well as individuals in society.

James's integration of individuals and institutions is signaled by his discussion of the university. As we have seen, he presents a balanced view of the university in several late lectures. He describes the university as an institution whose responsibility is toward the individuals who are a part of it. The university should support its geniuses in their education and research, and it should teach its non-geniuses how to discriminate between ideas, so that they will become good selectors. Conversely, individuals need the university. Geniuses are dependent on it for support; non-geniuses for training.

If James had written about the church at this point in his life, would he have adopted a more balanced view of it? Might he have argued that the church could play a role as vital to religion as the university plays to education? If the church were to give up its tendencies toward dogmatism and indoctrination, could it be an institution that supported geniuses in their education and experience of religion? Because religious geniuses are not created ex nihilo, the church might provide such person with information and experiences that could be crucial to their development. Might the church also train non-geniuses to discriminate wisely between religious ideas? Although religious experience seems to be more private for James than education, it is not unreasonable to suppose that roles such as these might be played by the church.

JAMES, EMERSON, AND KIERKEGAARD

So far in this chapter, I have stated the Integration Thesis, argued that it resolves tensions other methods of interpreting James cannot resolve, and shown how the move toward integration takes place in James's metaphysical, psychological, and sociological thought. The individualism that arises from James's integrated self brings together the volitional individualism of the *Will to Believe* and *Principles* and the perceptual individualism of *Varieties*. In this section, we will explore this individualism by comparing it to that of two other nineteenth-century individualists, Søren Kierkegaard and Ralph Waldo Emerson. These thinkers embrace, respectively, some form of the theism and idealism James identifies in *A Pluralistic Universe* as living rivals of his own radical empiricism. Although all three thinkers hold the individual to be irreducible and primary on the social level, we will see that only James's individualism is thoroughgoing and radical enough to maintain the irreducibility and primacy of the individual on the metaphysical level. Let us begin by exploring the similarities that exist on the social level among these three individualists.

Kierkegaard, Emerson, and James are all strongly individualistic in the social realm. That is, they defend the individual's independence from surrounding social conditions. Kierkegaard and Emerson would agree with James that individuals arise in a cycle of operation different from society. These thinkers hold that, however strongly individuals influence their social environment and are influenced by it, individuals are unique and not reducible to their social surroundings.

There are, however, at least two problems that arise from such individualistic views. First, the freedom individuals enjoy in their independence from society can become an isolating distance. The distance between individualism and loneliness is often not very great. Second, individualists must contend with the difficulty of human mortality. Those who feel themselves closely connected to their society can take comfort in the fact that it will survive their death. They can find great consolation in the belief that their union with the social whole does not terminate at death, since the effects of their life continue to be felt. Individualists, however, have less access to this consolation. For them, the distance between individuals and society may seem to be too great for the overcoming of the tragedy of death in this way. Thus, mortality is the great nihilistic threat to whatever importance individuals have apart from their society.

Since James seems to be more concerned with the second of these problems arising from individualism, it is the one we will focus on here. A typical individualistic solution to the problem of mortality is belief in a saving deity. James, Kierkegaard, and Emerson all try to solve the problem in this way.[10] Each makes a division between two worlds: the natural world and a larger spiritual world. For these thinkers, the natural world determines our ordinary, common understanding of life. The mortality that is such a threat to the individual belongs to this world. They also hold that the spiritual world is not as easy to see as the natural world. It usually requires some struggle to become aware of it. This struggle is rewarding in that it reveals a spiritual immortality that overcomes the mortality of the natural world.

At this point, the similarities shared by the three thinkers end. They each turn to a saving deity, but the deity to which each turns is vastly different from the others. In order to show the radical and thoroughgoing nature of James's individualism, it will be important to look briefly at the most salient differences among the spiritual worlds and saving deities to which these thinkers turn. We will find that, in the cases of Kierkegaard and Emerson, the individuality that obtains at the natural level cannot survive its own spiritual salvation. The Gods of Kierkegaard and Emerson are too large to allow the metaphysical survival of the individuality of the individual. Only James, with his finite God, can give an account that rescues the individual both from the Nothingness of nihilism and from the overwhelming Being of some allegedly salvific deity.

Even though Emerson is famous for advocating self-reliance, his individualism is the weakest of the three. Emerson claims that individualism is a function of the natural world view and maintains that the fullness of reality belongs to the spiritual worldview. For him, the natural world, with its finitude, is merely an apparent and illusory version of the spiritual world. Emerson writes, "the soul's scale is one; the scale of the senses and the understanding is another. Before the great revelations of the soul, Time, Space, and Nature shrink away."[11] And again, ". . . there [is] no bar or wall in the soul, where man, the effect, ceases, and God, the cause, begins."[12] Thus, on the metaphysical level, individuality is really an illusion. The apparent plurality of individual selves with which our world is populated is reduced, in the spiritual world, to the Over-soul—within which, according to Emerson, "every man's particular being is contained and made one with all other."[13] The self on which Emerson encourages our reliance is not our respective finite individual selves, but rather the single, all-encompassing Over-soul, the "Aboriginal Self."[14] From the perspective of the Over-soul, whose perspective, according to Emerson, is the true one, all is one and all is well. For Emerson, then, social individualism is saved by giving up all pretensions to metaphysical individualism.

Kierkegaard's individualism is quite different from Emerson's. For Kierkegaard, the natural world, in which we all begin, is a fallen one where there is no possibility of true individuality. In our natural state, we are each an undifferentiated part of the crowd. We have existence, but not yet essence. The only way anyone can acquire an essence, and thus become an individual, is before God. Kierkegaard identifies the will as the means to achieving this individuality. This implies that, from the human perspective, both individuality and religion are founded in volition. But volition, as we have learned from James, is temporally secondary to perception. Indeed, for Kierkegaard, the choice to become an individual before God is made possible only through God's revelation of truth that would otherwise be unavailable.

Individuality, for Kierkegaard, is divinely mediated, so that God is the guarantor, or at least the condition of possibility of individuality. This implies that individuality, wherever it exists, is derivative and dependent on God. Kierkegaard writes, "in relating to itself and in wanting to be itself, the self is grounded transparently in the power that established it."[15] But it is hard to see how individuality is the sort of thing that *can* be derivative. Just as a feudal nobleman, whose only chance at independence lies in the acquisition of land, actually gives up his independence if he accepts this land as a fiefdom from the king, so it seems that a derivative individuality is really the abnegation of individuality.

The divine help that Emerson and Kierkegaard find for the individual on the social level must be paid for on the metaphysical level. On the social level, these deities affirm individuality by helping the individual overcome the view of mortality as tragic, but on the metaphysical level, Emerson's deity renders individuality illusory and Kierkegaard's renders it derivative. Of the three views in question here, only James's radical empiricism can claim to preserve metaphysical individuality. Like Emerson, James locates individualism in the natural world. But, unlike Emerson, he sees the larger spiritual world as pluralistic and compounded from elements in the natural world. While both Emerson and Kierkegaard try to solve the problem of nihilism by postulating a radically other spiritual world from which salvation comes, James postulates a spiritual world continuous with and constituted by the natural world. For Emerson and Kierkegaard, the arrow of meaning goes from the spiritual world to the natural world; for James, the arrow goes in the opposite direction, as well. For James, the individual point of view is neither illusory nor derivative. Instead, it is real for us and contributes to the larger, spiritual view. This is because the most developed point of view for James is not the absolute view, but the Ultimate view—the view that results from a temporal process of unification (P, 78). Since God is in the process of becoming ever more knowledgeable and ever more powerful, we, with our moral struggles, can influence his development (WB, 55).[16]

It does not follow from the constitutive role James gives the individual in God's development that his God is merely ideal and thus incapable of being the source of religious experience. The relation of the individual to God is much like the relation of one single computer to the Internet. The Internet is a finite, pluralistic cooperation between computers that has far more information available through it than that which could be stored in any single computer. The Internet acquires its information through its constituent computers, yet can also give back to these computers information they would otherwise be unable to acquire.

One problem with this analogy is that James's individuals and God are conscious, whereas computers and the Internet are not. If *per impossibile* computers and the intellect *were* conscious, it would be possible for the information from any single computer to be taken up into the Internet's conscious memory and remain there, influencing the Internet's decisions long after that particular computer had ceased to function. This, analogically, is James's view of immortality.

The failure of the individualisms of both Emerson and Kierkegaard on the metaphysical level emphasizes the radical nature of James's individualism. It extends to the sociological, psychological, and metaphysical dimensions of his thought. Furthermore, James's mature individualism is an integrated one that emphasizes the interdependence of perception, conception, and volition.

A PRAGMATIC OBJECTION TO GALE

In the last chapter, I presented three objections to Gale's Divided Self Thesis. I argued that it is based on an unwarranted characterization of James as a mystical absolutist, that it intellectualizes the Promethean and the mystical aspects of experience, and that it ignores certain key texts that show strong support for an Integration Thesis. I made the case for my first two objections at the end of the last chapter. In this chapter, I have presented textual evidence for my Integration Thesis. If my objections are meaningful, they should make some important pragmatic difference. And indeed they do.

Gale's James is left singing "The Divided Self Blues" to the end of his days. But an integrated view—or better, perhaps, an integrating view—of James allows us to maintain the organic and developmental dynamism that is so important in his work. As the reflex arc indicates, personal growth is a function of graceful alternation between the active and the perceptual—between the Promethean and the mystical—phases of life. The biographies of many social geniuses would argue that the most satisfying type of meaning comes from a Promethean working out of a mystical calling. Cutting either out radically impoverishes the other.

A look at the practical results of Gale's Divided Self Thesis actually leads to a fourth objection to it—an objection that, from a Jamesian perspective, is more telling than any of the others. Gale sees the Promethean and the mystical as centrifugal forces that tear a psyche apart. If, instead, we see them as normal phases of a healthy life, we can consider the practical questions of how the Promethean can enrich the mystical and of how the mystical can enrich the Promethean. Making a turn of this sort will allow us to appreciate and extend the developmental dynamism in James's individualism. In the next and final part of this book, we will try to do just that.

We turn now to Part III, in which we will examine the "cash value" of the Integration Thesis by using it to discuss what I will call "epiphanic experience," a realm of experience James did not fully explore in his writings. We will find that the interplay of the Promethean and the mystical in this realm is not only possible, but also necessary for human flourishing.

PART III

An Application of the Dynamic Individualism of William James

CHAPTER 6

Structured Wholeness:
The Integration Thesis in Practice

In the previous chapter, I traced out some of the effects of James's gradual conversion. I argued that this conversion is a move toward the integration of various parts of his heterogeneous personality, and that it has significant effects on different aspects of his thought. In his metaphysics, it results in a theology that meets the needs of the individual for both meaning and intimacy. In his epistemology, it makes room for both percepts and concepts in a human understanding of the world. Described in psychological terms, the first of these two shifts in James's thinking represents an integration of perception and volition; the second, one of perception and conception. I also pointed out that James does not carry out this integration on all levels of his thought and that this presents us with the challenge of its further development.

In this chapter, I take up that challenge. Of course, there are a variety of ways in which this Jamesian project might be continued. The way I have chosen to develop, which I call "structured wholeness," is one I think has special promise. Based on the reflex action model, it ensures an essential place to each of the faculties of perception, conception, and volition and holds them to be interdependent. It gives us a way of seeing in a new light a problem James identifies in *Varieties* as being at the root of religious disagreements. Let's begin examining structured wholeness by taking up just this problem.

MOMENTS VERSUS AVERAGE RESULTS

The problem James identifies concerns the relative worth we assign to two different phases of experience, phases he refers to as "moments of sentimental and mystical experience" on the one hand, and "average results" on the other. More specifically, James writes:

> There are moments of sentimental and mystical experience . . . that carry an enormous sense of inner authority and illumination with them when they come. But they come seldom, and they do not come to every one; and the rest of life makes either no connection with them, or tends to contradict them more than it confirms them. Some persons follow more the voice of the moment in these cases, some prefer to be guided by the average results. Hence the sad discordancy of so many of the spiritual judgments of human beings. . . . (VRE, 22)[1]

What are we to make of these two phases of experience and of their frequent seeming opposition? Must those who experience both choose for one or the other, or is there a way of integrating them? In the case of religious geniuses, such an integration is not only possible but actual. Indeed, as we saw in chapter 3, and as we will observe in more detail later in this chapter, one of the defining characteristics of religious geniuses is an automatic transformation of average results based on moments of sentimental and mystical experience. For a religious genius, mystical moments are cases of ideomotor action, where internal transformation and sometimes external action follow immediately and without deliberation.

Not everyone, however, who experiences mystical moments can integrate them as easily with the average results as religious geniuses are able to do. Religious non-geniuses do not experience an automatic transformation of the average results based on the moment. Indeed, James himself is a good example of a religious non-genius. He is no stranger to "moments of sentimental and mystical experience," yet such moments are not automatically transformative for him.[2] In this chapter, I want to explore a solution to this problem based on the integrated individualism pointed to by the Integration Thesis we examined in the last chapter.

Before exploring this solution, though, I would like to flesh out the problem a bit. I believe the religious tension between moments and average results is a special case of a larger problem. Although some of these moments that "carry an enormous sense of inner authority and illumination with them when they come" are religious in nature, many are not. I propose the term "epiphany" to designate this larger class of moments, some—but not all—of which are religious. While this term itself has religious roots—referring to the manifestation of Christ to the gentiles through the visit of the Magi—I use it here in its broader, more contemporary sense of a sudden, intuitive manifestation of what feels to be essential reality or meaning.

The problem I would like to explore in this chapter is one regarding epiphanic experience and the integration of its two components. Specifically, I would like to ask how it is possible for an epiphanic non-genius (like James himself) to integrate epiphany with the mundanity to be found in the average results. The solution I will propose, structured wholeness, is based on the reflex arc. Not only are James's criteria for judging the value of a moment (immediate luminousness, philosophical reasonableness, and moral usefulness) based on the reflex arc, but so, too, I will argue, is the integrated cycle of epiphanic experience itself. Since the point of this chapter is to explore the integration of the two phases of epiphanic experience, it is important to begin by clarifying more specifically what I mean by epiphany and mundanity. That is the task of the next two sections.

EPIPHANY

A great writer on epiphanic experience is Ralph Waldo Emerson. Although he uses different terminology, epiphany is one of the major themes of his work. He writes of it often and contrasts it with what I have termed mundanity. One of his best descriptions of these two types of experiences occurs in his essay "Experience":

> In the street and in the newspapers, life appears so plain a business, that manly resolution and adherence to the multiplication-table through all weathers, will ensure success. But ah! presently comes a day, or is it only a half-hour, with its angel-whispering,— which discomfits the conclusions of nations and of years! Tomorrow again, everything looks real and angular, the habitual standards are reinstated. . . .[3]

In their extreme forms, these angel-whisperings become sudden intuitions that burst into our normal, everyday experience like revelations. They carry with them a sense of clarification, which seems to allow us to understand things in their true nature. Such epiphanies are

like bolts of lightning on a dark night that brilliantly illuminate everything in a single, instantaneous flash. There are many different kinds
of epiphanies. They can be religious, philosophical, romantic, aesthetic,
or some other type.

Accounts of religious epiphanies are common in sacred texts.
The experience of the Apostle Peter on the Mount of Transfiguration
is a quintessential example in the Christian tradition of a religious
epiphany.[4] It is difficult to imagine a revelation that would be more
satisfying for Peter. He has gone far out on a limb by quitting his job
to follow an unknown itinerant preacher around the country. He must
wonder from time to time, especially when the Jewish religious leaders are particularly harsh in their attacks on Jesus or when his own
stomach is growling unusually loudly, whether he is on the right track
or whether he is being duped by yet another false messiah. Then,
having made it into the inner sanctum, he is made privy to the secret
teaching—or, rather, to a secret experience.

Peter, James, and John accompany Jesus up a mountain. According to the biblical accounts, when they get to the top, Jesus is suddenly
transformed, and they are able to perceive his true nature. Jesus' clothes
become white as snow, his face bright as the sun. With him—speaking
to him, validating his messianic claims—are Moses and Elijah. At this
point, everything is clear in Peter's mind. All doubt is gone. The whole
world is illuminated. Peter wants nothing other than to stay on that
mountaintop forever. To ensure this, he offers to build three taber-
nacles: one for Jesus, one for Moses, and one for Elijah. But before
Peter can finish speaking, a voice out of a cloud confirms Jesus' divinity. Terrified by this voice, the disciples fall to the ground. The next
thing they know, the epiphany is over, and it is time to follow an
untransfigured Jesus back down into the valley.

Although the contents of philosophical epiphanies are different
from those of religious epiphanies, their results can be just as meaningful for those experiencing them. In the *Symposium*, Plato describes
a kind of philosophical epiphany, reached through what he calls the
ascent of love. This is a process in which one begins with the love of
the beauty of a single body and moves to beauties of ever greater
abstraction until "all of a sudden" one catches sight of the form of
Beauty itself. The epiphanic vision of Beauty then allows the soul to
give birth to true virtue.[5]

A more concrete example of a particular philosophical epiphany
can be found in the biography of William James. In chapter 1, I mentioned the depression James fell into as a young man upon the conclusion of his medical studies. A key to overcoming this depression was

a philosophical epiphany he experienced through reading essays written by the French philosopher Charles Renouvier. As noted previously, James writes of this experience: "I think that yesterday was a crisis in my life. I finished the first part of Renouvier's second *Essais* and see no reason why his definition of free will—'the sustaining of a thought *because I choose to* when I might have other thoughts'—need be the definition of an illusion" (LWJ, 147). Thus, this powerful epiphany, which changed James's life so dramatically, was based on philosophical insight.

Romantic epiphanies are, perhaps, the most elusive type of epiphany. No doubt all of us, at least at some point in our lives, long for the sudden revelation of another person as the perfect object of our romantic desires. Unfortunately, however, this revelation seems to be more an object of popular imagination than of actual experience. Shakespeare did much to popularize epiphany as the basis of romantic love. His Romeo and Juliet provide an example of a rare reciprocal romantic epiphany. When these characters first meet at a feast in Juliet's home, they both experience "love at first sight."[6] Unfortunately, romantic epiphanies seem more often to be one-sided, as Proteus sadly discovers in *The Two Gentlemen of Verona*.[7] Whatever the ultimate results of romantic epiphanies, they can be just as powerful as religious or philosophical ones, and they can affect our lives just as significantly.

Some epiphanies are principally aesthetic experiences. They can be brought about through the appreciation of natural beauty or of the arts. Although they are sometimes as powerful and life-changing as other kinds of epiphanies, they are often more limited bursts of appreciation of the beauty revealed in some particular area of our experience. William Wordsworth describes such a moment of aesthetic epiphany in his poem "Composed Upon Westminster Bridge, Sept. 3, 1802." He describes the effects of an early-morning view of London from Westminster Bridge as he is leaving for France:

> Earth has not anything to show more fair:
> Dull would he be of soul who could pass by
> A sight so touching in its majesty:
> This City now doth, like a garment, wear
> The beauty of the morning; silent, bare,
> Ships, towers, domes, theatres, and temples lie
> Open unto the fields, and to the sky;
> All bright and glittering in the smokeless air.
> Never did sun more beautifully steep
> In his first splendor, valley, rock, or hill;

Ne'er saw I, never felt, a calm so deep!
The river glideth at his own sweet will:
Dear God! the very houses seem asleep;
And all that mighty heart is lying still!

Whatever the type, epiphanies are an important kind of experience. To use a theological term, epiphanies are examples of grace. They are gifts of unmerited favor, whose presence we can neither fully earn nor completely control. The epiphanic wind bloweth where it listeth. Often epiphanies come when they are least expected and seem to be unconnected to the mundane reality that precedes them. Conversely, anyone who has tried to plan a perfect moment understands the difficulty of the task. The question of whether the source of this grace is divine can be put aside by admitting that its source is not totally within individual human consciousness.

There are two other characteristics of epiphanies that I should mention here. First, epiphanies often come with a sense of atemporality. During the experience, the subject usually has little sense of the passage of time, and, after the epiphany is over, the subject often has difficulty judging how long it actually lasted. A second characteristic of epiphanies is that they are temporary. The eternality belonging to the internal economy of epiphanies is, paradoxically, matched with an ephemerality that characterizes their external relations. The temporary atemporality of epiphanies is one reason why it is so difficult to know how to respond to them appropriately. The atemporality of an epiphany may well lead the subject to think it will last forever. But this is not what happens. However breathtakingly long a flash of lightning may last, it comes to an end. So, too, epiphanies are only moments. Upon realizing the temporary quality of an epiphany, the subject may well experience a sense of loss and even of betrayal, feelings that will influence his or her response to the epiphany and, ultimately, his or her interpretation of epiphanic experience in general. This is an important point to which I will return after I have described in more detail what I mean by mundane experience.

MUNDANITY

When an epiphany ends, we slip back into mundanity. Mundanity is the common, ordinary experience of everyday life. "Mundanity" should be understood denotatively here, without the added connotation of being boring and sterile. Of course, mundanity *can* be boring and sterile, if it remains unintegrated with epiphany. More generally, however, it is the everyday part of experience, the part that provides the rhythm of life. This is the part of life over which we feel we have a great deal of control, or at least with which we are very familiar. There is a certain feeling of safety that accompanies the mundane. This safety can, of course, become constricting and depressing, but it need not. We often take great pleasure in the repetition of simple tasks and tasks that have become simple for us through our mastery of them. In the mundane world, habit guides much of our behavior, and if we go beyond habit, we rely on careful, rational planning based on past experience.

The basic difference between epiphany and mundanity is that epiphany is characterized by wholeness, while mundanity is characterized by structure. Epiphany involves connection and insight. Heretofore unnoticed similarities become apparent and the entire world seems to present itself as a single, atemporal, all-encompassing unity. Mundanity, on the other hand, is highly structured. It is structured by habit and reason. It involves a high degree of analysis, with complex distinctions playing an important role. In epiphany, the similarities in the world tend to be seen as identities; in mundanity, they tend to be seen as differences. I do not mean to imply by this distinction that epiphany and mundanity are always clearly separated and mutually exclusive. They are on the same structure–wholeness continuum, with epiphany tending toward wholeness and mundanity tending toward structure.

Epiphany and mundanity can result in different views of the self, which, in turn, give rise to different types of individualisms. Views of the self based on epiphany are typically pantheistic, emphasizing the connection to the All; while views based on mundanity usually involve a more isolated self, emphasizing its separation from all else in the world. Emerson's individualism is based on the epiphanic self. For Emerson, the true self is the Over-Soul, the All. Although our mundane selves may divide us into individuals on the social level, from Emerson's metaphysical standpoint, this division is illusory. Many Eastern religions also emphasize the epiphanic self at the expense of the mundane self. A result of this emphasis is that the highest states in these religions tend to be structureless. An exclusive emphasis on the mundane self, on the other hand, can result in a solipsism in which there is no connection between the self and anything else in the universe. On this view, the mundane self is the only thing that occupies its universe. Since it is hard to find meaning in such a radically isolated, mortal self, it is difficult for such a view to escape nihilism.

Although James does not put it in these terms, his integrated view of the self avoids both the inarticulate unity to which the epiphanic self can lead and the solipsistic fragmentation to which the mundane self can lead. James avoids these extreme positions by including both the epiphanic self and the mundane self as interdependent components of the integrated self. The mundane self, for James, is dependent on the epiphanic self for a sense of meaning and connectedness; the epiphanic self is dependent on the mundane self for the texture that keeps it from collapsing into an inarticulate metaphysical unity. Thus, epiphanic connection gives meaning to mundanity, and mundane structure gives form to epiphany.

THE RESPONSE OF FAITH

I have already noted that epiphanies are momentary parts of the experiential flux. However permanent they may seem while we are experiencing them, sooner or later they are swept away by the same ebb and flow that brought them in the first place. Barring some specific response on our part, the habitual, non-epiphanic world will soon reassert itself, and even the memory of the epiphanies will fade into insignificance. Several types of responses to epiphanies are possible, and these responses profoundly influence the ultimate effect of epiphanies on our lives.

One possible response to epiphanies is not an active response at all. It is merely the forgetting of the experience, allowing it to fade away as quickly as it may. This is often our response to epiphanies that seem to require major and unwanted behavioral changes in our lives. It may also be the way we respond to the first epiphanies we experience. When, for example, the awkward loneliness of adolescence is miraculously shattered by a connection with other equally lonely adolescents, we may initially respond with joy and amazement. But when the euphoria wears off, we feel doubly awkward in our vulnerable state and welcome the habitual relations of distance that reestablish themselves. Even the memory of the connection is embarrassing, so we try not to think about it, until eventually we begin to doubt that the event occurred as we had originally thought.

The movie *The Breakfast Club* explores just such adolescent experience. When five students from different social groups within their high school are forced to serve out detentions in the same room one Saturday, they unexpectedly begin to discover each other as individual human beings with feelings and value. Although at the beginning, each student seems incomprehensibly strange to the others, by the end of the detention period, each has achieved an unexpected acceptance from the group. At this point, one of the students asks if they are all still going to be friends on Monday. Most of the students realize that the social pressure from their friends will be too great to overcome. From Monday's perspective, with the epiphany long over, their revelations will be embarrassments. As the days and weeks unfold, their epiphany will become a strange dream choked out by the return to the status quo. From Monday's position, it will be a relief when the memories fade and the temporary moment of connection is forgotten.

Youth camps and retreats provide further examples of intense moments whose memories become too awkward to sustain. In the excitement of the week, friendships are formed and religious and social commitments are made. But the mundanity of life as usual that is encountered upon returning home makes it exceedingly difficult to follow through with them. The easiest way to overcome the tension between the epiphanic week and the normality of everyday life is to try to forget the epiphany as soon as possible.

Another possible response to epiphanies is the active one of romanticism. Romantics[8] feel epiphany to be far superior to mundanity. They may also be especially sensitive to the shock that comes with the return from epiphanic clarity to the mundane world of everyday experience. Romantics try to avoid mundane experience and the shock that accompanies reentry into it by attempting to extend the epiphany. Finding a way to live the rest of one's life within the epiphanic moment would mean that the unsympathetic mundane world would no longer have to be taken into account. Peter's response to the transfiguration was typically romantic. He thought that, by some action on his part, he might induce the transfigured conversationalists to stay forever. This would allow him to remain on the mountaintop eternally, always face to face with the affirmation that his hopes and dreams, his beliefs and risks, were all justified. The problem with romanticism is that it does not work. As Peter quickly found out, epiphanies are not sustainable. They end, returning the romantic, kicking and screaming, to the mundane world.

Different romantics respond in different ways to this defeat. Some refuse to abandon the search for the never-ending epiphany, since they cannot imagine what other goal in life would be worth pursuing. They are like conquistadors who, knowing at some level that El Dorado does not exist, nevertheless persist in their exploration because finding it, they believe, is the only thing that could make life worth living. They are like gamblers who, knowing that the chances of winning the jackpot are negligible, nevertheless continue to try their luck in the belief that they could find happiness in no other way than in winning the big prize.

Other romantics comfort themselves with the thought that, although no particular epiphany is sustainable, it is possible to experience another epiphany like the one that has just gone. These romantics "live for the weekend." Knowing that the workweek cannot be escaped, they try to survive it by telling each other about previous weekend experiences and by making plans for future weekends. Some of these romantics try to guarantee an epiphany through drugs, sex, or danger. But these self-induced attempts at epiphany often result in addiction, where the rewards of a certain activity decrease over time, and the cost of indulging in it increases.[9]

A third response to epiphanies is that of cynicism. The name "cynic," understood in a contemporary rather than in a historical sense, applies to those who, like romantics, are overcome by the power of an epiphany at the time they are experiencing it. Unlike romantics, however, once the epiphany is over, cynics try to escape from the pain of its absence by ridiculing it, sometimes ridiculing even their own vulnerability to it.

Stoicism is a fourth response to epiphanies. Stoics refuse to vacillate in their estimation of the value of an epiphany. They are determined to distrust it not only after it is gone, but even when it is most strongly tempting them with its delights. Stoics reject epiphanies because they refuse to surrender themselves emotionally to experiences whose origin lies outside of their conscious control. Stoics may also reject epiphanies on the epicurean grounds that they are disruptive and bring pain in their wake. Because the euphoria of an epiphany is often succeeded by a depressing reentry into the mundane world, stoics may decide it is in their best interest to give up the joy if they can in this way also avoid the pain.

Beyond the passive response of simply ignoring and forgetting the experience, romanticism, cynicism, and stoicism constitute three very different active responses to epiphany. Romanticism rejects the mundane world outside of the epiphany, stoicism rejects the epiphany itself, and cynicism accepts the phase of experience in which it happens to be and rejects the other. Each of these responses tries, in its own way, to eliminate the experiential tension accompanying the vacillation between epiphany and mundanity. Despite this intention, the result of each is actually to increase the tension by refusing to value all of experience. I believe a far more promising way of dealing with the initial tension is to try to lessen it through a volitional integration of the two phases of experience. Such an integration must affirm both the epiphanic and the mundane as essential to the self. As James says of the related notions of percepts and concepts, "We need them both, as we need both our legs to walk with" (PU, 34). Because I take faith to be key to the integration of the epiphanic and the mundane, I call this integration the response of faith.[10]

Responding in faith to an epiphany means valuing both epiphany and mundanity. It is a decision to trust epiphanies both while they are happening and after they are gone, as well as a choice to make the most of mundanity. While persons of faith do not require the infinite extension of the epiphany itself, they choose to extend the epiphanic view of the world into their mundane lives. That is, they choose to live their mundane lives as though the epiphanic view of the world is correct. For them, mundanity is not a negative phase of experience; rather, it is what makes possible the appropriation of epiphany. As we will see later, persons of faith also understand that mundanity, through the volitional process of hope, can have an influence on epiphany, as well.

Augustine's response to the epiphany of his conversion is a good example of what I mean by the response of faith. After his conversion in the garden in Milan, Augustine decides to reinterpret his whole life in light of it. Augustine's reinterpretation, recorded in his *Confessions*, along with the more general working out of his salvation, is not an automatic response to his conversion; instead, it is a result of his active response to it in faith.

From this vantage point, we can see that the key terms of epiphanic experience—epiphany, mundanity, faith, and hope—correspond to the three elements of the reflex arc. The receptive experience of epiphany corresponds to perception, the rational and habitual mundane world corresponds to conception, and the mediating elements of faith and hope correspond to volition.

Because religious experience is a subclass of epiphanic experience, many of James's conclusions about religious experience also hold for epiphanic experience. I have stressed the connection between these two types of experiences by noting the theological analogues of the various parts of the self involved in the integration of epiphanic experience. Epiphany corresponds to grace, mundanity corresponds to reason, and the will that integrates them may best be understood in terms of faith and hope. In the next section, I will explore more of the similarities between religious and epiphanic experience. Understanding the relations among grace, reason, and the faith and hope that integrate them will help us understand the relations among the analogues of these terms in the context of the broader human experience we are examining.

THEOLOGICAL ANALOGUES

Theology has long held faith and reason to be in opposition. It has claimed that their opposition centers around the nature of our access to truth. Is the truth about the world to be found through faith in divine revelation, or is it to be found by rational means? Thomas Aquinas tries to solve this problem by dividing truth into three categories. He argues that some truths, such as the doctrine of the trinity, are accessible only through revelation. Other truths, such as the truths of science, are not part of God's special revelation and so can be known only through reason. Still other truths, such as those of natural theology, can be accessed either through revelation or through reason.

The traditional opposition between faith and reason can be reinterpreted, in light of its epiphanic analogue, in a way that I believe is truer to experience. According to this reinterpretation, the opposition is really between grace and reason, which represent two different types of experiences. The novelty of epiphany is often contrary to the habitual views of mundanity. Some people choose to reconstruct their mundane worlds in the light of novel experience, while others choose to interpret epiphany in accordance with more habitual ways of seeing the world. Indeed, this is the difference—noted by James in the quotation we examined at the beginning of this chapter—between those who follow the "voice of the moment" and those who prefer the "average results."

The old opposition between faith and reason, reinterpreted as an opposition between grace and reason, shows faith to involve a choice between epiphany and mundanity. Living in the light of grace means trusting our own epiphanies or those of others reported to us by persons we trust. Choosing reason means guiding our lives in accordance with mundanity, which includes both rational thought and habits based on past experience. In more general terms, the question is whether to make decisions about the future based more on present experiences or on the habitual distillation of past experiences.

Although the relation between grace and reason is often one of opposition, the relation between grace and faith seldom is. Except in rare cases when faith rejects epiphanic grace, the presence of grace obviates the need for faith. Aquinas holds a similar view concerning the relation between knowledge and belief. He argues that it is impossible for there to be knowledge and belief in one person concerning the same object. For example, Aquinas holds that it is possible, by means of faith in authority, to *believe* that God exists or, by means of rational demonstration, to *know* that God exists. But he claims that, having attained to a *knowledge* of God's existence, it is not possible for a person at the same time to *believe* in God's existence. My claim concerning grace and faith is similar. I contend that epiphanic certainty renders faith impossible. Epiphanies carry with them such a sense of certainty that volitional effort plays no role in their acceptance.

In terms of James's psychology, we can say that epiphanies are cases of ideomotor action, cases in which outgoing nerve currents are stimulated automatically and not deliberately. The only way volitional effort can be involved here is not in their acceptance, but in their rejection. Indeed, stoics demonstrate that it is possible, by a volitional choice, to reject an epiphany as it occurs. Although I believe that the stoic rejection of epiphanies is inappropriate, I also believe, as I will show in the last section of this chapter, that there are times when the volitional rejection of a particular epiphany *is* appropriate. In cases where the epiphany is not rejected, however, it is only when the experience is over and the attendant involuntary certainty is gone, that faith has a role to play in keeping the memory of the epiphany from fading away.

This exploration of the theological analogues of epiphany, mundanity, and their volitional integration shows that epiphanic experience resembles religious experience in many ways. There is, however, at least one important difference between my view of epiphanic experience and James's discussion of religious experience in the *Varieties*. I will explore that difference in some detail in the next section.

ESCAPING ELITISM

In chapter 3, I argued that James's focus on religious geniuses renders his discussion of religious experience elitist. I noted that, according to James's own psychological account, the experience of geniuses is very different from that of others, since their unusually focused attention makes volition relatively less important for them. I concluded that James's emphasis on the religious experience of geniuses is one reason for the dislocation of volition in the *Varieties* and that it provides an obstacle to the application of James's discussion to the religious experience of non-geniuses. Structured wholeness avoids the problems that arise from this elitism by taking a different approach. Instead of focusing on the experience of epiphanic geniuses, it emphasizes the experience of epiphanic non-geniuses, in which volition is not dislocated. Because the distinction between epiphanic geniuses and epiphanic non-geniuses is such an important one, it will be worthwhile to explore it in more detail.

There is a sense in which all persons who experience epiphanies might be considered epiphanic geniuses. Involuntary attention *during* an epiphany is a common characteristic of all epiphanic experiences. However, the term "epiphanic genius" will be more meaningful if it is reserved for those for whom involuntary attention *follows* the epiphany, as well. For epiphanic geniuses of this narrower sort, there seems to be no need of a volitional response to the epiphany. Their involuntary attention results in an automatic mundane appropriation of epiphany. Some examples will help to clarify what I mean.

I will take two examples of epiphanic genius from the *Varieties*. The first example is of an Oxford graduate, who describes his conversion and then writes of its effects as follows:

> From that hour drink has had no terrors for me: I never touch it, never want it. The same thing occurred with my pipe: after being a regular smoker from my twelfth year the desire for it went at once, and has never returned. So with every known sin, the deliverance in each case being permanent and complete. I have had no temptation since conversion. . . . (VRE, 182)

The second example is of a similar case, where the results of the converting epiphany were sudden, automatic, and permanent. At the close of the meeting in which the subject was converted, he went out on the street. He describes what he experienced there in the following way:

> I met a gentleman smoking a fine cigar, and a cloud of smoke came into my face, and I took a long, deep breath of it, and praise the Lord, all my appetite for it was gone. Then as I walked along the street, passing saloons where the fumes of liquor came out, I found that all my taste and longing for that accursed stuff was gone. . . . My appetite for liquor never came back. (VRE, 217)

Although these examples may seem rather simplistic, it is due to the automatic reordering of the mundane world that accompanies them that I consider them to be illustrative of epiphanic genius. The experience of epiphanic non-geniuses may sometimes seem more profound, but it lacks this automatic reordering of the mundane world.

There are at least three reasons why the reordering of the mundane world might be blocked in the experience of non-geniuses. The epiphany may be vague, it may be ambiguously received, or there may be resistance to its appropriation. In the case of vagueness, there is doubt about what an epiphany means and about what effect it should have on the mundane. Although James does not focus on such cases, he does give some examples of them early in the *Varieties* in order to establish that many persons believe in the reality of entities they have felt spiritually but never perceived physically. One writer describes such an experience as follows:

> Quite early in the night I was awakened. . . . [I] felt a conscious-ness of a presence in the room, and singular to state, it was not the consciousness of a live person, but of a spiritual presence. This may provoke a smile, but I can only tell you the facts as they occurred to me. I do not know how to better describe my sensa-tions than by simply stating that I felt a consciousness of a spiri-tual presence. . . . I felt also at the same time a strong feeling of superstitious dread, as if something strange and fearful were about to happen. (VRE, 58)

Another example of an epiphany whose effects are blocked by vague-ness comes from the correspondence of James Russell Lowell, who writes:

> I had a revelation last Friday evening. . . . I never before so clearly felt the Spirit of God in me and around me. The whole room seemed to me full of God. The air seemed to waver to and fro with the presence of Something I knew not what. . . . I cannot tell you what this revelation was. I have not yet studied it enough. But I shall perfect it one day, and then you shall hear it and ac-knowledge its grandeur. (VRE, 61)

In these cases, the vagueness of the experience makes it unclear what response, if any, is appropriate. Thus, as Lowell indicates, appli-cation of the epiphany can only follow its volitional interpretation.

A second way the application of an epiphany can be blocked for non-geniuses is through its ambiguous reception. During the epiphany, its meaning and trustworthiness may seem perfectly clear. After it is over, the meaning may remain, but the trustworthiness may be in doubt. A good example of this case is given by C. S. Lewis in *Till We Have Faces*.

In this, his last novel, Lewis retells the myth of Cupid and Psyche. In Lewis's version of the myth, Psyche, the daughter of the king of Glome is sacrificed to a god, known as the Shadowbrute, in order to end a drought that has descended on the land of Glome. She is taken up to a mountain and left alive there, shackled to a tree, as a bride for the god. Orual, Psyche's half-sister, tries unsuccessfully to save her from this fate. Devastated by her failure and by her sister's tragic destiny, Orual becomes so sick she cannot even accompany her sister on her final journey. Days later, having at last recovered from her sickness, the only thing Orual can do is to go to the mountain to bury her sister's remains.

Upon reaching the mountain, however, Orual finds, not her sister's remains, but her sister, alive and well. Psyche tells Orual how she was freed from her shackles by the god of the West Wind and taken to the Shadowbrute's palace to be his bride. When Psyche tries to show Orual the palace, however, it becomes clear that Orual is incapable of seeing it. Moreover, in place of the robes Psyche thinks she is wearing, Orual sees only rags. When Psyche gives her sister what she believes are wine and honeycakes, Orual sees only water and wild berries. Orual thinks her sister must be deceived, yet Psyche's sincerity and obvious well-being, more in keeping with living in a palace than with camping out in a lonely mountain valley, make Orual wonder whether she herself is not the one who is deceived.

That night, Orual sleeps on the other side of the river from where Psyche alleges her palace to be. In the middle of the night, Orual goes to the river for a drink—and sees the palace just as Psyche has described it. It is so unexpected a thing that Orual wonders if she should trust her senses. A little while later, the fog swirls in, and the palace is hidden from view. At the end of Orual's epiphany, there is no question what she *seems* to have seen. The doubt that plagues her is whether, in fact, she *has* actually seen it. If the palace is really there, Psyche's story must be true. If not, Psyche is deluded and in danger of freezing in the approaching winter.

In Orual's case, the epiphany is not vague at all. If the experience is trustworthy, she knows quite clearly what it means and how she should respond. The ambiguity here is a function, not of the epiphany's meaning, but of its trustworthiness. Did Orual really see the god's palace, or did she, in her fatigue and confusion, really see only fog? Epiphanic ambiguities of this sort can only be resolved volitionally.

A third way that the application of an epiphany can be blocked for a non-genius is through the resistance of habit or desire. In these cases, the epiphany may be quite clear in its meaning, and its trustworthiness may persist after it ends. Yet because its application would require the breaking of old habits or the denial of desire, it can be appropriated only volitionally.

This difficulty is clearer to Aristotle and to the Apostle Paul than it is to Plato. For Plato, to know the Good is to do it. Aristotle, on the other hand, writes:

In self-restrained and unrestrained people we approve their principle, or the rational part of their souls, because it urges them in
the right way and exhorts them to the best course; but their nature
seems also to contain another element beside that of rational principle, which combats and resists that principle. Exactly the same
thing may take place in the soul as occurs with the body in a case
of paralysis: when the patient wills to move his limbs to the right
they swerve to the left; and similarly in unrestrained persons their
impulses run counter to their principle.[11]

Paul too makes much of the experience of not doing what one knows
one ought to do. Whatever later interpreters have theorized about the
nature of Paul's converting epiphany, he himself seems never to have
been in doubt about the meaning of his experience on the road to
Damascus. There is apparently no question in Paul's mind that the
vision was of the very Christ whose followers he was persecuting, nor
is there any record that Paul subsequently doubted the trustworthiness
of the experience. Neither vagueness nor ambiguous reception are at
issue here. Yet Paul's own confession of the blocked effects of his conversion show that, in the sense in which I am using the term, he is not
a religious genius. After his conversion, Paul writes: "I find . . . a law,
that, when I would do good, evil is present with me. For I delight in the
law of God after the inward man: But I see another law in my members,
warring against the law of my mind, and bringing me into captivity to
the law of sin which is in my members."[12] I will not pretend to give a
full exegesis of this difficult biblical passage. My point here is merely
that the mundane appropriation of epiphany in this case is blocked in
its execution, not because of the vagueness or ambiguity of the epiphany,
but because of the habits and desires of mundanity.

Having explored some of the differences between the experience
of epiphanic geniuses and that of epiphanic non-geniuses,[13] I will now
turn to the presentation of structured wholeness. Because this theory
is based on the experience of epiphanic non-geniuses, it takes epiphany,
mundanity, and the will to be equally important and interdependent
parts of the experience of the healthy human self.

STRUCTURED WHOLENESS

The integration of epiphany and mundanity by means of faith does
not result in a static, homogeneous kind of experience. Instead, experience continues to be dynamic, but the phases of experience are no

longer in violent opposition, as they often are without such integration. This integration is a praxis that requires mature judgment if its execution is to be successful. One must first be able to judge whether one is in an epiphanic or in a mundane phase of experience, since each phase places different requirements on the individual. Because epiphanies are of varying value, one must also be able to judge the value of a particular epiphany and the extent to which it should be appropriated by the mundane self.

I believe the appropriate attitude to have during an epiphany is the natural one of receptivity. In those rare and powerful disruptions of everyday experience in which the whole world seems to lie at our feet in euphoric clarity (as well as in the more common and less powerful epiphanies), we should simply give ourselves up to the experience. Any active response at this point is not only difficult, but improper. This is not to say, however, that an active response is *never* appropriate. To everything there is a season. Moments of grace are unsustainable. They will end. The light will fade. The sense of community will slip away. The overwhelming feeling of truth will leave. We will return to the same mundane world we inhabited before the epiphany. It is after the epiphany is over that our active response is not only appropriate but crucial.

The first response that is required of us is the judgment of the value of the epiphany. Not all epiphanies are created equal. Like the cardinality of transfinite sets, they are all infinite, but not necessarily to the same degree. Unlike the cardinality of transfinite sets, though, they can be either infinitely positive or infinitely negative. It is faith's role to decide whether an epiphany will be accepted as positive or rejected as negative. This decision is not an arbitrary act of the will, and the main value of the decision is not the act of the will in itself, but rather the appropriate use of the will.[14] There are certain criteria that can help the will to make a good judgment about an epiphany, and it is possible for the will to err.

Although he does not seem to make much use of them, James does mention—as we noted earlier—three criteria for the exercise of faith. They are immediate luminousness, philosophical reasonableness, and moral usefulness (VRE, 21-3). Immediate luminousness is the immediate feeling of the experience, philosophical reasonableness is the consistency of the experience with other beliefs we already have about what is true, and moral usefulness is the serviceability of the experience for our moral needs. In this way, present, past, and future experience are taken into account, as are perception, conception, and volition.

While all epiphanies cross a certain threshold of emotional infinity, once across that threshold, each has its own degree and quality of immediate luminousness. In accordance with James's criterion, the more intense and pure the feelings of a particular experience, the more worthy of faith it is. Similarly, a high degree of philosophical reasonableness tends to evoke a high degree of faith. Peter's experience on the Mount of Transfiguration had a high degree of philosophical reasonableness for him. Because the Transfiguration confirmed so many things he already believed to be true about Jesus, the likelihood seemed high that the epiphany was trustworthy, and he placed great faith in it. Finally, epiphanies that correspond with what we consider to be ethical have a high degree of moral usefulness and so deserve more faith. For example, an epiphanic vision of a peaceful and racially integrated world would, because of its moral implications, deserve a higher degree of faith than one of an ethnically cleansed world.[15]

Earlier in this chapter, I mentioned that there are occasions in which the rejection of an epiphany as it occurs may be appropriate. That is, although receptivity is usually the appropriate attitude toward epiphanies, there are some cases in which an active rejection of the epiphany as it begins to occur may be more appropriate. These are cases where it is readily apparent that the epiphany has a negative content, perhaps because the subject has experienced a similar epiphany in the past. Such cases of immediate rejection of epiphanies differ from stoicism in that they are based on a judgment about the content of a particular epiphany. Stoic rejection of epiphanies is a rejection of this type of experience in general and has nothing specifically to do with the contents of any particular epiphany. Thus, this modification does not change the essence of my position. There may be some rare instances in which faith should decide on an immediate rejection of a particular epiphany. Usually, however, receptivity is the appropriate attitude to have during an epiphany, with faith deciding the appropriate response to it after it is over. It is this more usual case that I will focus on here.

In normal cases of epiphanic experience, after the epiphany is over, faith judges the extent to which the epiphany is to be accepted. It is to this extent that the experience must be processed by the mundane self. Faith overcomes the opposition between epiphany and mundanity by a process of integration that transforms mundanity into appropriation. Without epiphany, there would be no experience to process; yet without the appropriative act of mundanity, the experience would never become our own. Appropriation is a process by which the wholeness of an epiphany enters into the structure of our mundane lives. It is the process of spiritual digestion. It is grace seeking understanding. It is a spiritual incarnation, where epiphanic infinity is incarnated into mundane finitude. Without appropriation, an epiphany remains a wholeness that will quickly fade away because it is so foreign to our particular, finite selves.

There are many paths appropriation can take as it rearranges the habits of our everyday lives in the light of epiphanic experiences. Common to all of these ways, however, is memory. The principal thing is that epiphanies not be forgotten. The way to ensure this is through the building of memorials. Memorials can be concrete, physical structures like plaques, parks, and statues, or they can be mental constructs.

The former type of memorial is illustrated by a story recounted in the Hebrew Bible.[16] According to this story, the Israelites, after forty years of wandering in the wilderness, are finally ready to cross over the Jordan River into Canaan, the land flowing with milk and honey. But the Jordan is flooded and presents a great obstacle to their arrival in the Promised Land. As has happened so often on their journey, Jehovah once again works a miracle. As soon as the priest's feet touch the water, the Jordan's flow is stopped and the people are able to cross on a dry riverbed. After all the people have crossed over, Joshua, in accordance with Jehovah's command, tells a representative of each tribe to take a rock from the riverbed and place it on a pile as a memorial of the miracle that has occurred that day. When future generations of children see the pile of rocks and ask why it is there, their parents are to tell them about the crossing of the Jordan on dry land. This is not a romantic attempt to prolong the miracle. The Jordan resumes its normal flow, and the miracle is over. The point is rather to prolong the *memory* of the miracle in faith. This memory provides strength for the present and hope for the future.

Dostoyevsky, in *The Brothers Karamazov*, gives us an example of the construction of a mental memorial. Alyosha, the youngest of the Karamazov brothers, effects a reconciliation between a group of schoolboys and one of their colleagues named Ilyusha. Ilyusha is taken ill and, after a long illness, dies. At the end of the book, Dostoyevsky describes Ilyusha's touching funeral, which Alyosha and the boys attend. In the very last scene, Alyosha talks with the boys after the funeral. The biblical allusion is made clear by the fact that the boys, like Jesus' disciples, number exactly twelve. Alyosha tells them there is nothing "higher, stronger, more wholesome and more useful in life than some good memory." He continues, "And even if only one good memory is left in our hearts, it may also be the instrument of our salvation one day."[17] Alyosha challenges the boys never to forget the epiphanic moment that has been brought about by Ilyusha's death. He urges them never to forget the feelings of love and tenderness they feel for Ilyusha, for him, and for each other, since the preservation of this single memory can keep them from becoming evil and heartless later in life.

Whether a memorial is a physical or a mental construct, it forms an important part of the appropriative response to epiphany. This response, in which faith works itself out in the structure of the mundane world, can be of various kinds. Religious responses usually involve theology, a theoretical account intended to explain how and why religious epiphanies occur and what they mean. Great emphasis is placed on a tradition of memorials, with the faithful assenting to the given interpretation of them. Sometimes the social aspect of religion and the theoretical component of theology are stressed at the expense of the actual epiphanies from the past that are to be memorialized, as well as of the new epiphanies experienced by adherents of the religion. A religion becomes a tyrannical dogma when memorials are more important for it than epiphanies.

This points out one of the dangers of memorials. They must be strong enough to ensure the preservation of the memory of the epiphany, but they must not become so strong and wooden that they squeeze the life out of the memory and disallow other epiphanies from occurring. Consider the case of a man who is amazed by the size and beauty of a certain oak tree. Afraid that something might destroy the tree, he decides it must be protected. He designs a wooden building to protect the tree's life. Knowing the strength of oak, he fells the tree and uses its wood to construct the building. Thus, the very act intended to protect the tree is the act responsible for its destruction. Wood is, indeed, essential to the life of a tree, but it must be "living" wood. It must be wood that delivers required materials to the leaves and provides necessary support. Analogously, memorials must preserve the memory of a living epiphany and not try to replace it with an ossified, lifeless structure.

Appropriative responses to epiphany can also be philosophical. Philosophy emphasizes a rational understanding of the meaning and function of epiphanies as a basis for their practical appropriation. The present chapter is one example of a philosophical appropriative response to epiphany.

Romantic epiphanies evoke romantic appropriations. When two people experience a mutual romantic epiphany, they usually want to reorder their lives so they can share as much of themselves with each other as possible. The traditional way in which this is accomplished is through marriage.

A final appropriative response is aesthetic. While religion emphasizes a memorial tradition and philosophy stresses rational structure, art is an intuitive and sensuous response to epiphany. Light, sound, space, and time are used in expressive ways to represent and interpret the original experience.

To this point, the arrow of influence has gone from the epiphanic to the mundane, from wholeness to structure. I have tried to show how epiphanies, accepted in faith and duly appropriated, result in a structural change of the mundane and a concomitant modification of behavior. Earlier in this chapter, I pointed out that the arrow of influence goes in the opposite direction, as well. Mundane structure can also influence epiphanic wholeness. James makes analogous claims in both his metaphysics and his epistemology.

In his metaphysics, as we saw in chapter 5, James holds that the human and the divine influence each other. As humans, we influence God, since we are constitutive elements of his consciousness. God, in turn, influences us through the revelations of religious experience.

In his epistemology, as we also saw in chapter 5, James finds a similar relation of mutual influence between percepts and concepts. In *Some Problems of Philosophy*, he writes: "Perception awakens thought, and thought in turn enriches perception. The more we see, the more we think; while the more we think, the more we see in our immediate experiences, and the greater grows the detail and the more significant the articulateness of our perception" (SPP, 59). That is, percepts influence concepts, since they are the original experience from which conceptual translations are made. Concepts, in turn, influence percepts by making us more aware of what we are perceiving.

It is important to note the precise nature of these metaphysical and epistemological relations. They are relations of influence and interdependence, but not of determination. James's universe, it must be remembered, is not a block universe; rather, it is one where there is pluralistic play between its parts. Although, on the metaphysical level, James holds that we are constitutive of God's consciousness, we no more determine him, on James's view, than the sensory images constitutive of our consciousness determine us. Nor, for James, does God determine us through religious experience. Such experience certainly influences us strongly, but we are free to choose how we will respond to it. On the epistemological level, there is similar play in the relations between percepts and concepts. Like all translations, conceptualization is an interpretation.[18] As such, it is neither exhaustively accurate nor completely determined by perception. Conversely, the enhanced perceptual awareness brought about by concepts in no way amounts to a relation of determination. No amount of piecing concepts together, in James's view, will yield a percept.

The relation between epiphany and mundanity in structured wholeness is similar to these relations in James's metaphysics and epistemology. Epiphany and mundanity influence, but do not determine, each other. Structured wholeness holds that no appropriation is completely adequate to epiphanic experiences and that no amount of mundane restructuring is sufficient to guarantee an epiphany. It will be worthwhile to explore in more detail the precise nature of these relations between epiphany and mundanity.

We have already seen that mundane appropriation is influenced by epiphany. Like conceptualization, appropriation is a structural translation of experience. As a translation, no appropriation is ever completely adequate to the particular epiphany it translates. The appropriation of an epiphany involves memory, analysis, and restructuring. It involves remembering the experience, breaking it apart in some way in order to understand it, and restructuring our mundane lives in accordance with it. In each step of this process, we lose part of the epiphany. The memory of an event never attains to the fullness of that event, analysis never captures its object completely, and restructuring is never free of all distorting resistance. This does not mean, however, that appropriation should be abandoned. Just as James argues that, despite its failures, conceptualization is one of the most important human capabilities, so appropriation, despite its limits, is an essential part of integrated human experience.

The arrow of influence between epiphany and mundanity is reversed when the analysis of epiphany, carried out as far as it can, gives way to synthesis. Synthesis is a creative reorganization and construction using the structural elements acquired through analysis. It is of great importance in making structural preparations for epiphany. These preparations involve an invitation of epiphany and also affect the contents of epiphany when it does come. Synthesis is like the building of an altar from stones we quarry during analysis. We build this altar in the hope that fire will come down from heaven to consume our sacrifice. These preparations do not guarantee that the fire will come. If it does not, we must not feel betrayed; if it does, we must not feel we have earned it. We make our preparations as an invitation and in order to make the best use of whatever gifts we receive. Even so, with time, we can become more adept at this process, increasing the likelihood that our preparations will be efficacious.

The life of Augustine furnishes us with an example of the value of synthesis. In the *Confessions*, he writes that a reading of Cicero's

Hortensius awakens in him a love of wisdom. His ensuing search for wisdom takes him through Manichaeanism and Neoplatonism before it results in his famous Christian conversion in the garden in Milan. Although he does not know exactly what he is searching for, he reads extensively and tries to order his learning and his experience to bring him as close to wisdom as possible. This ordering amounts to a synthesis of his mundane experience in evocation of and preparation for epiphany. Without this synthesis, without his lengthy and difficult search for wisdom, he would not have experienced his conversion in Milan—or if he had, the experience would have been far less rich. Through this lengthy process of synthesis, Augustine develops a mundane structure that not only evokes the epiphany, but also helps define it when it comes.

If synthesis is the reverse process of appropriation, then hope is the reverse of faith. While faith is the decision to modify the mundane world in accordance with epiphanic insight, hope is the decision to evoke the epiphanic world through mundane action. Just as the appropriation called for by faith is never completely adequate to experience, so the synthesis called for by hope cannot completely control epiphany. Whatever the degree of freedom the restructuring impulse is given in our mundane lives, it is never sufficient to guarantee an epiphany. Just as, despite its failure, appropriation must not be given up, so synthesis must not be abandoned, even though it always falls short of its goal.

The relations of mutual influence that hold between epiphany and mundanity show that the integration in structured wholeness is not static; rather, it is a dynamic process of the evolution of the self. This takes us back to the beginning of our study. In chapter 1, we examined James's discussion of the similar process of social evolution. We saw that, in his account of social evolution, James applies the selection model to the social relations among individuals. For James, social evolution works itself out in terms of the relations of interdependence between geniuses and non-geniuses. Non-geniuses are dependent on geniuses for creative suggestions, and geniuses are dependent on non-geniuses for their selection. From our present vantage point, after a dialectical turn inward, we can see how personal evolution functions in a similar, although slightly more complex, way. Personal evolution is a function of the self's alternation between epiphany and mundanity. This alternation, which involves relations of mutual influence between epiphany and mundanity, is mediated by the will. When epiphany influences mundanity, faith mediates; when mundanity influences epiphany, hope mediates.

The same point can be made using the very similar reflex action model. In the case of epiphanic non-geniuses, the translation of percepts into concepts is not automatic; nor is the move from concepts into volitional action. Through faith, an epiphanic non-genius can appropriate a perceptual epiphany in a way that transforms the conceptual. Similarly, through hopeful volitional action, such a person can evoke further perceptual epiphanies. Thus, personal growth is a function of volitional mediation between the perceptual and the conceptual, between epiphany and mundanity.

This brings into clearer light the pathology of the romantic, cynical, and stoic responses to epiphany. Each of these responses tries to drive a wedge between the crucial phases of existence we have identified.

By accepting epiphany and rejecting mundanity, romantics convert the dynamic relations of mutual influence into static, dualistic ones of acceptance and rejection. They do not see the role mundanity can play in enriching epiphany, and their consequent rejection of it impoverishes the very epiphany they value so highly.

A stoic response to epiphany leads to similar consequences. By rejecting epiphany out of hand, stoics protect themselves, not only from danger and disappointment, but also from the life-giving revelations of epiphanies. Stoics are like patients in a hospital who, afraid of the bacteria that might be in their food, refuse to eat. Because of this refusal, they forfeit the energy the food would have provided for fighting off bacterial infection, and they lose the life-sustaining nutritional value of the food, as well. The fear that controls the actions of stoics not only cuts them off from the joys of epiphany, but it also impoverishes the mundane world within whose confines they attempt to live their lives.

Although cynics, it is true, accept both epiphany and mundanity, they do so by turns. Their acceptance of one always involves the rejection of the other. Thus, the practical results of cynicism are similar to those of romanticism and stoicism. The rejection of the alternate phase of experience leads to a rejection of the influence the two phases can have on each other and results in a painful, halting alternation between the two that impoverishes both.

In contrast to these pathological responses, structured wholeness works toward health through integration. This integration respects the integrity of each phase of experience, but recognizes the potential each has for enriching the other. Epiphany can enrich mundanity through faith, and mundanity can enrich epiphany through hope. In a healthy, integrated self, the alternation between epiphany and mundanity is not one of violent opposition. Nor is it merely circular. The relations of mutual influence result in an upward spiral into ever greater richness and complexity. Thus, through these dynamic relations, as described by structured wholeness, the self is freed to enjoy limitless progress.

Conclusion

I began this book with the observation that it would be difficult to dispute the claim that William James is an individualist. At this point, that claim seems all the more difficult to deny. Our study has confirmed that James is an individualist throughout his writings on social philosophy, psychology, and metaphysics. I also claimed that it was important to get clear on the kind of individualism James espoused. Our study has shown that this is not as easy to ascertain. As I end this book, I am mindful that the systematic study of this central aspect of James's thought is by no means complete. I intend to have opened a new thread of conversation among those interested in James's thought. I hope others will take up the conversation, expanding and critiquing the account I give here. Such a conversation will show that James is not merely a "champion of sheer individuality." Rather, he is a defender of a highly nuanced and rich individualism that promises important rewards to those who study it carefully.

Incipient though it is, our study has nevertheless yielded some important results. It has made clear that James's individualism is dynamic in at least three different ways. First, James's individualism has a diachronic trajectory. In his early writings, James espouses a volitional individualism; in this middle writings, a perceptual individualism; and in his late writings, an integrated individualism. In James's early and middle works, his individualism is out of balance and full of tension. His sociological descriptions of religious institutions, his psychological descriptions of the faculties of the spiritual self, and especially his descriptions of religious experience, tend to subordinate reason and emphasize either volition or perception. In his late works, as a result of his gradual conversion, James begins to resolve some of these tensions. He develops a metaphysics that stresses both perception and volition, defends an epistemology that values both perception and conception, and softens his anti-intellectualism and his anti-institutionalism. The result is a more integrated and balanced individualism that stresses the equal importance and interdependence of perception, conception, and volition.

Integrated as James's individualism becomes, though, it remains radical. That is, it reaches to all dimensions of his discussion of the self. It is at work on the social level in his argument that geniuses arise from a cycle of operation different from their environment and in his (qualified) defense of every individual's freedom of belief; it is apparent in his psychology in his claim that psychology is properly the study of finite, individual minds and in his claim that every thought tends to be part of a particular personal consciousness; and it is expressed metaphysically in his preference for personal, private religion and in his argument that individual human selves are constitutive of the divine consciousness

As we have noted, the radicality of James's individualism sets it apart from other individualisms. Emerson and Kierkegaard are two of the most noted individualists of the nineteenth century, yet we have seen that neither develops an individualism as radical as James's. Emerson's individualism, so strong on the social level, does not survive metaphysically, since, on this level, the pervasive unity of the Over-soul renders individuality illusory. Kierkegaard's individualism, although quite different from Emerson's, also fails to achieve the radicality of James's. For Kierkegaard, it is true, individuality persists on both the social and the metaphysical levels, but the radicality of his position is vitiated by the derivative nature of his individuality. Kierkegaard's individual, who is *derived* from God, is less radical than James's individual, who is *constitutive* of God.

It may at first seem oxymoronic to characterize something as both integrated and radical. In the case of James's individualism, however, the need for integration is a function of its radicality and the success of its radical pretensions is predicated on their integration. Without integration, James's individualism would be too full of tension to be tenable; without radicality, there simply would be less of a need for integration.

Beyond its diachronic dynamism, James's individualism, as we have seen, is also organically dynamic. Because for James an individual is constituted physiologically by a reflex arc, the same dynamism present in the reflex arc is to be found in the Jamesian individual. The movement of nerve currents through the reflex arc from perception to conception to volition is precisely the movement that defines a healthy individual. Although different experiences may emphasize one or another of these elements, any interpretation of James that involves a severing of their connections—or, worse, the excision of one of the elements—is bound to be unsatisfactory and dangerous. Unsatisfactory because it is not an accurate reflection of James's views; dangerous because it works against the third sense of dynamism to be found in James's individualism.

This third way in which James's individualism is dynamic is in its orientation toward growth. In this way, it is developmentally dynamic. For James, the self is essentially a process of unification. We are continually becoming something we never were before, and this requires a continuous search for the truth that will unify new facts and old beliefs. Put physiologically, incoming nerve currents modify existing neural networks and result in new outgoing nerve currents. This process naturally results in growth, and, by exercising our wills effectively, we can enhance and manage this growth.

In accordance with James's own pragmatic test of truth, an idea is true insofar as it leads to positive results in practice. Thus, the best argument for James's individualism is the contribution it makes to the enhancement of growth in the individuals it describes. This is a further reason why I disagree so strongly with nondynamic interpretations of James's individualism. More than simply theoretically inaccurate, they work against enhanced human growth and flourishing.

I hope it is clearer now, for example, why I object so strongly to Gale's reading of James. This is no idle dispute in the history of philosophy. It is a matter that concerns each one of us—or at least each of us who feels the tension between the Promethean and the mystical. Gale's Divided Self Thesis intellectualizes the problem and leaves us with nothing practical to do but attempt to assuage the resulting pain by singing the blues. My Integration Thesis keeps the tension concrete and encourages explorations of ways of helping the Promethean and the mystical find mutually supportive roles. Indeed, the final chapter in this book has been just such an exploration. By finding positive and creative ways to integrate the pragmatic and the mystical in our lives, we can avoid the fate of having to hop, now on our pragmatic foot, now on our mystical foot. If we learn to move gracefully between these two important phases of experience, we will in effect have learned to walk. With time, we may even learn to dance. When that happens, we may well want to trade in our blues for swing.

Notes

INTRODUCTION

1. Perry, *Thought and Character,* 265.
2. Danisi, "Vanishing Consciousness," 3.
3. Smith, *Spirit of American Philosophy,* 41.
4. McDermott, *Streams of Experience,* 44.

CHAPTER 1

1. We now know, of course, that certain environmental factors such as radiation increase the likelihood of mutation. Nonetheless, environmental conditions—or at least our knowledge of them—are still inadequate to explain why a particular mutation occurs in a particular cell. See Seigfried, 1990, 83.

2. This last argument seems rather weak, as James does not consider that the strategic geographical placement of Sicily, a placement that both Corsica and Sardinia lack, has had a strong influence on its history. Nor does he consider that, in Napoleon, Corsica has produced a dramatic leader who has changed the course of world history far more than any Sicilian leader has. For present purposes, however, assessing the strength of James's particular arguments is less important than grasping their value for understanding his individualism.

3. The scientific veto resembles the *sola scriptura* of the Protestant reformation and the criterion of meaning of the Vienna Circle. Just as the reformation cry of *sola scriptura* is not to be found in the Scriptures and the criterion of meaning itself is meaningless according to its own criterion, so the scientific veto requires its own vetoing, because it is not scientific.

4. Euclid, *Elements,* 251.

5. James's distinction between theoretical and practical matters reflects his ambivalence to categories that I mentioned in the first section of this chapter. James's distinction is useful, but, if pushed too far, will collapse. As a pragmatist, James believes that all meaningful theoretical propositions have practical consequences. In fact, the meaning of a theoretical proposition is nothing other than its practical consequences. Thus, insofar as a geometrical theorem is meaningful, it cannot be exclusively theoretical. A geometrical

theorem can be used as an example of a "theoretical proposition" only in the sense that its direct practical consequences are not as great as those of "practical propositions" like those concerning the purchase of fire insurance.

6. Russell, *Western Philosophy*, 815.

7. Why did James choose exactly these three characteristics as constitutive of genuine options? The requirement that the hypotheses be living seems easy to understand. In fact, it seems to be more of a descriptive than a prescriptive rule, since dead hypotheses are not ones we would be tempted to believe in the first place. Perhaps James requires genuine options to be momentous because there are simply too many living, forced options for us to consider carefully. We can deliberate only the most important ones. The requirement that an option be forced seems more difficult to understand. Whether an option is forced seems to have more to do with the way the option is formulated than with any state of affairs in the world. Avoidable options can be reformulated as forced ones. Take the example, "Human beings were created by God," versus "Human beings are a result of evolution." This option is not forced, since it is possible not only to believe the first or the second hypothesis, but to believe both or neither, as well. That is, it is possible not only to be a creationist or an evolutionist, but also to be a theistic evolutionist or to believe, for example, that human beings are themselves divine and thus without origin. This avoidable option between creationism and evolution can be reformulated as two forced options: "Human beings were created by God," versus "Human beings were not created by God"; and "Human beings are a result of evolution," versus "Human beings are not a result of evolution."

8. See, for example, Perry, 1935, I, 320–32; Allen, 1967, 162–70.

9. Mark Hopkins (1802–1887) was a well-respected and popular American educator. He was a spirited teacher and lecturer, president of Williams College from 1836 to 1872, and the author of a number of books on morality and religion.

10. It is interesting that James's thesis when talking to an audience of women is that the value of a college education should "help you to know a good man when you see him." Beyond the ambiguity raised by the gender reference, we can see that there is no talk here of *being* a genius, but only of *recognizing* and *supporting* one.

CHAPTER 2

1. This is similar to Peirce's fallibilism. H. S. Thayer points out that for Peirce a "confession of inaccuracy and one-sidedness' incorporated within a belief (or statement) is 'an essential ingredient of truth' " (1981, 127). Furthermore, the absence of a fallibility factor would mean, for Peirce, that our beliefs would put an end to all our doubts and thus end our inquiry completely (1981, 128). Thayer further notes that Dewey followed Peirce in taking the idea

of "confessed inaccuracy" quite seriously "not only as a condition of the truth of assertions but also as an essential characteristic of scientific method" (1981, 128). But he does not mention the role that fallibilism plays for James.

James argues that conceptualization is crucial for rational beings, but that we must never forget the fallibility of our conceptions. He expresses this fallibility as the fringe that surrounds our thoughts. His self-avowed purpose is to reinstate the vague to its proper place (PP, 246); that is, to remind us that conceptions are never completely accurate and infallible.

There are two reasons why James's process of conceptualization is an ongoing one. First, our experience is in constant flux, and our conceptualizations of it must be modified to reflect these changes. Second, the fact that our conceptualizations are never fully accurate requires their continual fine-tuning.

William Joseph Gavin quite rightly makes much of James's discussion of vagueness and conceptualization in his book *William James and the Reinstatement of the Vague* (1992). We will return to Gavin and to this discussion in chapter 4.

2. James first published what he here calls the second and third characteristics of thought in 1884 in an article entitled "On Some Omissions of Introspective Psychology" (reprinted in EP, 142–67). The notion of continuity they presuppose anticipated Peirce's work on continuity by more than ten years. At the time James was writing that the continuity of perception is not composed of discrete automatic parts, Peirce held the nominalistic, Cantorian view that a continuum is composed of a transfinite set of points. It took Peirce more than ten years to develop an alternative definition of the continuum that does not include Cantor's nominalism. See Potter and Shields (1977) for an excellent overview of the development of Peirce's understanding of continuity.

3. James leaves this characteristic out of his account in the *Briefer Course* (PBC, 140).

4. Those interested in doing so may consult Capek (1953), among others.

5. See the exchange of letters between Thomas Davidson and William James reprinted in Perry (1935) 1:734–9.

6. This notion that reason is neither primary to the other faculties nor independent of them is at the basis of James's later development of pragmatism. James is especially frustrated by the emphasis of the then-prevailing German idealism on knowing. Like Marx, he believes that the main point is not merely to know, but to change the world. Reasoning must be firmly based in the world of real problems that confront us, and it remains so much idle speculation unless it helps us to solve those problems. Truth, for James, is nothing other than thoughts that prove effective in solving such problems.

7. Readers familiar with John Dewey's (1896/1998) article "The Reflex Arc Concept in Psychology" are aware that Dewey is quite critical of the reflex arc. He argues that it ought to be replaced by the notion of a circuit, since "the motor response determines the stimulus, just as truly as the sensory stimulus determines movement" (p. 6). Although Dewey puts this point more forcefully than James would, and although Dewey no doubt makes more of this

issue than James would prefer, I do not think James would have any trouble assenting to a circuit model. It is as if James is giving a "snapshot" of the interaction of the various elements of the psyche and Dewey is arguing for the "movie version."

8. This is similar to Aristotle's contention that *ousia* is the ultimate reality from which *idea* and *hyle* can be abstracted.

9. It should be noted that James makes this distinction between sensation and perception only in *Principles*. Elsewhere, James uses these terms synonymously. In his later works, James employs the latter term almost exclusively. He means by it direct, concrete experience as opposed to the discrete, abstract conceptual processing of that experience. See Gavin's (1992) related insightful discussion of "The Ontological Status of Percepts and Concepts" (pp. 64–9).

Gerald E. Myers writes on this point, "The official claim of Jamesian psychology is that sensations cannot fuse; former psychological explanations of such fusion are replaced by James's hypothesis that a specific sensation is the first psychic event to follow required events in the brain. If there is any reason to invoke fusion to explain sense-perception, James supposes the fusion to be a process in the brain rather than a psychological one. . . . [Despite] James's appeal to [his *esse est sentiri* doctrine] in *Principles*, he had difficulty in always adhering to it. His account of how the perception of space is acquired seems at crucial places to desert the official view of *Principles* and to claim instead that sensations can fuse" (1986, 87–8). Nowhere in his discussion does Myers take note of James's comment in his discussion of imagination. James writes, "An imagined object, however complex, is at any one moment thought in one idea, which is aware of all its qualities together. If I slip into the ordinary way of talking, and speak of various ideas 'combining,' the reader will understand that this is only for popularity and convenience, and he will not construe it into a concession to the atomistic theory in psychology" (PP, 691).

10. At least, this is James's pragmatic claim. It is not easy to determine to what extent a pragmatic judgment of truth is possible. If truth is what works, how can we judge what works? Bertrand Russell claims that the answer to this question involves an infinite regress. The judgment that something works is a true one only if the judgment itself works. We can determine whether the judgment works only by means of a further judgment, which, in turn, calls for another judgment, and so on ad infinitum (1945, 817).

11. This process of perceiving a thing's essence is explained somewhat differently by Peirce through his concept of abduction.

12. Julius Bixler's claims concerning the significance of the phenomenological experience of effort for James are problematic. Bixler's claims are as follows: Radical empiricism says that whatever is in experience is real; but James holds that "volition is an indubitable fact of experience"; thus, James concludes that freedom must be real (1926, 68).

Bixler's interpretation is problematic both because it leads to logical problems and because it is not accurate to James's writings. First, difficulties arise if we are not careful to distinguish properly between what is real and what is true. It is correct to say, for James, that whatever is in experience is real, but it does not follow from this that he holds all our conclusions about our experience to be true. According to James, since volition is an indubitable fact of experience, it follows that the *feeling* of freedom is real; but it does not follow, as Bixler seems to claim, that the freedom itself is real, since that would be tantamount to claiming the truth of our freedom based on the reality of our feeling of freedom. This kind of argument, if accepted, would validate not only our claims to freedom, but also every delusional conclusion of the mentally insane that is based on a real sensation.

Bixler's conclusion also runs contrary to James's own arguments. In discussing the question of freedom of the will, James is careful to note that feeling something to be true does not necessarily make it so. He even gives an example to make his point. In the case of effortless volitions, he argues, we have the feeling of freedom when we are not, in fact, free. It follows that we cannot legitimately argue from the fact that our wills *feel* free to the conclusion that our wills are free (PP, 1175–6). But this is precisely what Bixler seems to try to do.

13. Bixler misses this distinction when he writes that "the idea of the creative activity of consciousness is dominant" in *Principles* and that this book is "one of the most convincing scientific descriptions ever written of the essentially creative function of the human organism" (1926, 11). Had Bixler written "selective" instead of "creative," he would have been correct.

Patrick Dooley quite correctly points out that "in James's account voluntary action is but another example of the selectivity of consciousness.... [W]illing is not accomplished by initiating a special current of energy, but by the selection of ideas by attention" (1974, 58). Dooley does not go on to draw the conclusion that a selective will of the sort James describes cannot be a creative will.

14. Bixler seems to miss this point, as well, claiming that the question of freedom is a problem in James's psychology. Bixler correctly observes that "psychology was for James essentially a study of the mental process of selection." But then he goes on to claim that this shows that the problem of freedom is an important one in James's psychology (1926, 70–1). Actually, one of the strong points of James's scientific psychology is precisely that it is equally convincing whether or not our wills are free. The fact that James argues that we can "leave the free-will question altogether out of our account" (PP, 1179) shows that the question of freedom is not a problem for his psychology at all.

15. Kant, *Foundations*, 9–22.

16. I do not mean to imply that James agrees with Kant in every aspect of his theory. Kant stresses that moral action must be motivated from duty, whereas James does not place this requirement on the origin of moral effort. James's contribution is his psychological explanation of voluntary effort, which, when applied to Kant's theory, allows us to understand the latter in a more reasonable manner.

17. It may be that through repeated efforts of this sort, we develop a habit of acting. In this case, the course of action that was initially more difficult now becomes the easier course of action, and action in accordance with

it is no longer, strictly speaking, moral. We can say that we are acting in accordance with a good habit, a habit that was established through volitional effort; but action in accordance with a good habit is not moral action.

CHAPTER 3

1. Bixler, *Religion*, 4.
2. Ibid., 13.
3. James labels stoic resignation to necessity (i.e., moralism) as passive in comparison with the passionate happiness of Christian saints. He writes that the former is an example of the "defensive" mood; the latter of the "aggressive" (VRE, 41–2). Elsewhere, James calls the moral attitude "tense and voluntary," and contrasts it with religious surrender, where "[p]assivity, not activity; relaxation, not intentness, should be now the rule" (VRE, 95). In still another place, James identifies R_1 with action and R_2 with relaxation (VRE, 109). Clearly, the case is too complicated to allow a simple identification of one or another of these views with action or with passion.
4. Bixler is not completely consistent in this identification. In spite of himself, he writes, toward the end of his book (1926, 192), that R_1 involves relaxation, but he does not seem to realize how radically this conflicts with his earlier description of it (1926, 12–13, 16).
5. Douglas Anderson claims, quite rightly, that belief is not "legitimately consummated" until it includes all three faculties. Anderson holds that a worldview is degenerate as long as it does not account for all three (1989, 114).
6. A comparison between Kierkegaard and James on the difference between morality and religion would no doubt be instructive. Kierkegaard identifies three "stages along life's way": the aesthetic, the moral, and the religious. Although James explicitly mentions only two of them, his theory can easily accommodate the third. The aesthetic, the stage James does not directly mention, would be the non-genius's following of involuntary attention; the moral is the exertion of voluntary attention; and the religious corresponds to the genius's following of involuntary attention. Put differently, the aesthetic is the struggle to attain personal goals, the moral is the voluntary struggle to attain cosmic goals, and the religious is the attainment of personal goals through surrender to the cosmic.

Like Kierkegaard, James places religion higher than morality. Kierkegaard, however, stresses the reason in morality and the will in religion, whereas James stresses the will in morality and the surrender in religion. While Kierkegaard stresses the voluntary response to religious experience, James stresses the receptive nature of the experience itself. Furthermore, although Kierkegaard does not give a test to discriminate between good and bad religious experience, James does give one in *Varieties*.

Finally, it is instructive to note that James is an observer of religious experience, who claims not to have had any of his own. Kierkegaard, on the other hand, is a participator in, as well as a commentator on, religious experience.

7. See VRE, 172; see also VRE, 124, 140, 385, n. 2 and Perry, 1935 (2: 333).

8. The case James cites as that of a "French correspondent" (VRE, 134–5) is actually his own (Perry, 1935, 2: 324).

9. It should be kept in mind here that James is talking of only one strand of theism—scholastic theism. This means that he is taking theism as theology and not as religion. It also means that his discussion, and particularly his critique, really addresses scholastic theism and not theism in general. But perhaps, given the context of the Hibbert Lectures, that is sufficient. James is interested, after all, in addressing only those hypotheses that are living for himself and his audience.

10. Plato, *Parmenides*, 130.

11. More important, for present purposes, than Fechner's views is what James makes of these views. For this reason, my discussion of Fechner follows closely James's discussion in *A Pluralistic Universe*. Those interested in Fechner's metaphysics in its own right may consult him directly.

12. James does point out later that Fechner's all-enveloping God runs into the problem of evil (PU, 132–3). In trying to solve this problem, Fechner actually argues for a theistic God of a Leibnizian sort, who is placed under conditions of metaphysical necessity. James charges Fechner with intellectual laziness, whereas his formal position is monistic, while his practical position is pluralistic.

James himself might be accused of intellectual laziness at this point, since he fails to note that some of the same arguments that tell against Fechner's absolute God apply to his earth soul, as well, even if pluralistically construed. The earth soul appears to be nearly as unable to extricate itself from the problem of evil as is the absolute God.

13. James takes this term from Peirce, for whom it should be taken to refer to nonnominalistic notions of continuity, notions at which he arrived in the mid-1890s. See Potter and Shields (1977).

14. Elizabeth Flower and Murray Murphey make a similar point when they write that radical empiricism "extends the model of the stream of consciousness to metaphysics" (1977, 662).

CHAPTER 4

1. Seigfried, *Radical Reconstruction*, 10.

2. This is Peirce's term, quoted in Ruf (1991, xv).

3. This argument predicts the failure of any Cartesian project of taking the world, or our knowledge of it, apart into clear and distinct ideas and then trying to rebuild it again. James writes, "When you have broken the reality into concepts you never can reconstruct it in its wholeness. Out of no amount of discreteness can you manufacture the concrete" (PU, 116).

4. Gavin, *Reinstatement*, 91.

5. Ibid., 193.

6. Suckiel, *Pragmatic Philosophy*, ix–x.

7. Suckiel, *Heaven's Champion*, 88.

8. Seigfried, *Radical Reconstruction*, 10–15, 64.

9. Cooper, "Unity of William James's Thought," 114.

10. See, for example, Cooper's comments where he tries to separate James's philosophy from his biography, indicating his greater interest in "James's philosophical system" than in his "psychological frailties" (2002, 33–4).

11. Gale, *Divided Self*, 25.

12. Ibid., 16.

13. Ibid., 16.

14. In his introduction, Gale identifies that pragmatic value of belief in God or the Absolute to be a license to "take a moral holiday or feel safe and secure because all is well" (1999, 18). But this is the pragmatic value of mystical beliefs about God. The pragmatic value of Promethean beliefs is that it helps us access our deeper powers.

15. Gale, *Divided Self*, 19.

16. Bixler, *Religion*, 3.

17. Gale, *Divided Self*, 22.

18. Ibid., 253–4.

19. Ibid., 254.

20. Ibid., 255.

21. I am grateful to John Capps (2003) for helping me express this point more clearly. Capps was concerned that I seemed (in an earlier draft) to be saying, in my first objection, that James is not a mystic and then to be addressing the question, in my second and third objections, of how James's mysticism might be integrated with his pragmatism. The key, of course, is that in my first objection I deny James was a full-fledged mystic and that in my second and third objections I address the question of the integration of James's pragmatism with his lower-level mysticism.

22. Suckiel, *Pragmatic Philosophy*, 6.

23. Gale, *Divided Self*, 156–159.

24. Gale, "Still Divided Self," 157.

25. Gerald E. Myers, "Introduction," in *Talks to Teachers*, edited by F. H. Burkhardt (Cambridge: Harvard University Press, 1983), xi–xxvii.

26. For other passages on this matter, see PP, 1134–5 and TT, 25–6, 27–9.

CHAPTER 5

1. Even Bixler notes three stages in James's concept of God, with the third being an integration of the other two (1926, 122–36). Bixler's description of the three stages is not completely accurate, nor does he make much of the integration. Nonetheless, his account is an important step in the right direction. Curiously, he apparently fails to see the inconsistency between this step and what he says about James's religious conflict in the first chapter of his book (pp. 6, 17). There he contrasts "active pluralism" with "passive monism" and claims that James opts for pluralism.

2. It would be foolish to claim, of course, that no theists do, in fact, find meaning and comfort from their beliefs in God. I am simply trying to explicate James's argument that traditional orthodox theology is at odds with such meaning and comfort. I am not here intending to pass judgment on the validity of that argument.

3. It would certainly be surprising if the God of radical empiricism were gendered. In using gender-specific language here, I am merely following James's convention.

4. Here is an interesting related question: If James's God consists of the ideal part of the universe, is there a devil that consists of the evil part of the universe? To my knowledge, this is a question James never addresses directly.

5. This does not mean, of course, that James holds all the tenets of traditional empiricism. He agrees with traditional empiricism that concepts follow percepts but disagrees with it in his characterization of the type of percepts concepts follow. For James, percepts are not only of objects, but also of relations. He claims he is in no need of external relations to bind percepts together, since he holds relations to be intrinsic to the percepts themselves. He also departs from traditional empiricism in his belief that necessary truths are a result of natural selection and not of perception (PP, 1215–80).

6. Cf. "Reflex Action and Theism," in which James claims our main advantage over animals lies in our subjective and not in our rational aspects. He writes, "Man's chief difference from the brutes lies in the exuberant excess of his subjective propensities,—his pre-eminence over them simply and solely in the number and in the fantastic and unnecessary character of his wants, physical, moral, aesthetic, and intellectual" (WB, 104).

7. I leave aside here questions regarding the extent to which some animals may be capable of some level of conceptualization.

8. It is difficult to soften the contradiction between this passage and the one I quoted from page 31, which continues "but we have no reason to suppose that their immediate life of feeling is either less or more copious than ours." If our conceptions allow us to see more in our immediate experiences, it seems that our immediate life of feeling is certainly more copious than that of animals. Perhaps James could be excused on the basis that by "immediate life of feeling" he means pure sensation as described in *Principles*; whereas, by "immediate experiences" he means perception as distinguished from pure sensation. This seems to me a dubious, although not impossible intention. Another somewhat dubious but not impossible explanation for the apparent contradiction is that James's death prevented him from completing the book.

9. This might also be seen as the place of integration between mind and body, an integration that James makes controversially explicit through introspections that result in the claim that the central self is at least felt as physical movements. James's solution to the mind–body problem, however, is not within the focus of this present work, so I must leave its elaboration and discussion to another place.

10. Nietzsche is the outstanding example of a nineteenth-century individualist who does not stress the connection of the individual with a greater

deity. Not surprisingly, an important theme of his work is a struggle against nihilism.

11. Emerson, *Emerson's Essays*, 193.

12. Ibid., 192.

13. Ibid., 189.

14. Ibid., 46.

15. Kierkegaard, *Sickness unto Death*, 43.

16. This suggestion, which appears in *The Will to Believe*, shows that James long held that human actions could affect God. It is only with his account of the self-compounding of consciousness in *A Pluralistic Universe*, however, that he shows *how* this might occur.

CHAPTER 6

1. By "spiritual judgment," of course, James does not mean anything specifically religious. He simply means the value we judge something to have (see VRE, 13).

2. As with virtually all Jamesian categories, it is important to see the distinction between religious geniuses and religious non-geniuses as lying along a continuum. Specific persons are more or less religious geniuses to the extent to which their responses to religious experiences are automatic. Of course, the reflex arc guarantees that at least some *minimal* response is automatic, but geniuses go far beyond the minimum here.

3. Emerson, *Emerson's Essays*, 308–9.

4. Biblical accounts of this experience can be found in Matthew 17:1–9 and Mark 9:2–10.

5. Plato, *Parmenides*, 210A–212B.

6. William Shakespeare, *Romeo and Juliet*, in *The Riverside Shakespeare*, edited by G. Blakemore Evans (Boston: Houghton, 1974): 1.5.41–144

7. William Shakespeare, *The Two Gentlemen of Verona*, in *The Riverside Shakespeare*, edited by G. Blakemore Evans (Boston: Houghton, 1974): 2.4.99–214; 4.2.1–133.

8. It is an unfortunate fact about the English language that the adjective "romantic" can be derived from either of the nouns "romance" or "romanticism." Romantic epiphanies are, of course, epiphanies that involve romance, whereas a romantic response to an epiphany amounts, to some degree at least, to an embrace of romanticism.

9. For an insightful account of the process of addiction, see C. S. Lewis's *The Screwtape Letters* (1941/1982, 41–2, 55).

10. I do not use "faith" in a particularly religious way here. Of course, religious faith can be a response to a religious epiphany, but there are many other kinds of epiphanies. By "faith" I simply mean a trust in the epiphany, of whatever sort it might happen to be.

11. Aristotle, *Nicomachean Ethics*, I. xiii. 15–16.

12. Rom. 7:21–3 (The King James Version).

13. Significant as these differences are, it is probably best to place epiphanic geniuses and epiphanic non-geniuses on a continuum. The more one's response to epiphany is automatic, the more one is an epiphanic genius; the less one's response is automatic, the less one is such a genius.

14. I here intend to distance myself from a Kierkegaardian view of the will as arbitrary and especially from the view, adopted by some of Kierkegaard's followers, that the deciding, and not the content of the decision, is all-important.

15. The term "moral" must be understood pragmatically here. An act is immoral, not because it conflicts with some authoritative moral code, but rather to the degree that it hinders the flourishing of humans and of other living beings.

16. Josh. 3:7–4:24.

17. Dostoyevsky, *Brothers Karamazov*, 911.

18. See Gadamer, *Truth and Method*, 346.

Bibliography

WORKS BY JAMES

All works by James except *Correspondence, Letters,* and *Memories and Studies* are contained in *The Works of William James.* Edited by Frederick H. Burkhardt, Fredson Bowers, and Ignas K. Skrupskelis. Cambridge: Harvard University Press, 1975–1988. The original date of publication is given in parentheses.

The Correspondence of William James. Edited by Ignas K. Skrupskelis and Elizabeth M. Berkely, with the assistance of Bernice Grohskopf and Wilma Bradbeer. 12 vols. Charlottesville: University Press of Virginia, 1992–2004.

Essays in Psychology, 1983

Essays in Religion and Morality, 1982

The Letters of William James. Edited by H. James. Vol. 1. Boston: Atlantic Monthly Press, 1920.

Memories and Studies. New York: Longmans, 1911.

A Pluralistic Universe, 1977 (1909)

Pragmatism, 1975 (1907)

The Principles of Psychology, 3 vols., 1981 (1890)

Psychology: Briefer Course, 1984 (1892)

Talks to Teachers on Psychology, 1983 (1899)

Some Problems of Philosophy, 1979 (1911)

The Varieties of Religious Experience, 1985 (1902)

The Will to Believe, 1979 (1897)

WORKS BY OTHERS

Allen, Gay Wilson. *William James: A Biography.* New York: Viking, 1967.

Anderson, Douglas R. "An American Argument for Belief in the Reality of God." *Philosophy of Religion* 26 (1989): 109–18.

Aristotle. *Nicomachean Ethics*. Translated and edited by H. Rackham. Cambridge: Harvard University Press, 1934.

Augustine. *The Confessions*. Translated by Rex Warner. New York: Penguin, 1963.

Bixler, Julius Seelye. *Religion in the Philosophy of William James*. Boston: Marshall Jones, 1926.

Capek, Milic. "The Reappearance of the Self in the Last Philosophy of William James." *Philosophical Review* 62 (1953): 526–44.

Capps, John. Comments on James Pawelski's "William James on Crossing the Internal Divide: A Reply to Richard Gale." Unpublished manuscript read at the annual meeting of the Society for the Advancement of American Philosophy. Denver, Colorado, 2003.

Clifford, Willard K. "The Ethics of Belief." *Lectures and Essays*. 1879. Reprint, New York: Macmillan, 1886.

Cooper, Wesley E. *The Unity of William James's Thought*. Nashville: Vanderbilt University Press, 2002.

Danisi, John. "The Vanishing Consciousness." *International Philosophical Quarterly* 29 (1989): 3–16.

Dewey, John. "The Reflex Arc Concept in Psychology." In *The Essential Dewey*, edited by L. A. Hickman and T. M. Alexander. 2 vols. 1896. 3–10. Reprint, Bloomington: Indiana University Press, 1998.

Dooley, Patrick Kiaran. *Pragmatism as Humanism: The Philosophy of William James*. Chicago: Nelson-Hall, 1974.

Dostoyevsky, Fyodor. *The Brothers Karamazov*. Translated by David Magarshack. 1880. Reprint, New York: Penguin, 1982.

Eddington, Arthur, Sir. *The Nature of the Physical World*. Cambridge: Cambridge University Press, 1928.

Emerson, Ralph Waldo. *Emerson's Essays: First and Second Series Complete in One Volume*. New York: Harper, 1951.

Euclid. *The Elements*. Translated by Sir Thomas Heath. 2nd ed. Vol 1. New York: Dover, 1956.

Fechner, Gustav Theodor. *Religion of a Scientist: Selections from Gustav Theodor Fechner*. Translated and edited by W. Lowrie. New York: Pantheon, 1946.

Flower, Elizabeth, and Murray G. Murphey. *A History of Philosophy in America*. Vol 2. New York: Capricorn, 1977.

Gadamer, Hans George. *Truth and Method*. 1975. Translated and edited by Garret Barden and John Cumming. Reprint, New York: Crossroad, 1982.

Gale, Richard M. *The Divided Self of William James*. Cambridge: Cambridge University Press, 1999.

———. "The Still Divided Self of William James: A Reply to Pawelski and Cooper." *Transactions of the Charles S. Peirce Society* 40 (2004): 153–70.

Gavin, William J. *William James and the Reinstatement of the Vague.* Philadelphia: Temple University Press, 1992.

Kant, Immanuel. *Foundations of the Metaphysics of Morals.* 1785. Translated by L. W. Beck. Reprint, New York: Macmillan, 1985.

Kierkegaard, Søren. *The Sickness unto Death.* 1849. Translated by A. Hannay. Reprint, New York: Penguin Books, 1989.

Kuhn, Thomas S. *The Structure of Scientific Revolutions.* 2nd ed. Chicago: University of Chicago Press, 1970.

Lewis, C. S. *The Screwtape Letters.* 1941. Reprint, New York: Collier, 1982.

———. *Till We Have Faces.* 1956. Reprint, San Diego: Harcourt Brace, 1984.

McDermott, John J. *Streams of Experience: Reflections on the History and Philosophy of American Culture.* Amherst: University of Massachusetts Press, 1986.

Myers, Gerald E. Introduction. In *Talks to Teachers,* edited by F. H. Burkhardt, xi–xxvii. Cambridge: Harvard University Press, 1983.

———. *William James: His Life and Thought.* New Haven: Yale University Press, 1986.

Pawelski, James O. "William James and Epiphanal Experience." In *Religion in a Pluralistic Age: Proceedings of the Third International Conference on Philosophical Theology,* edited by D. A. Crosby and C. D. Hardwick. 277–88. New York: Peter Lang, 2001.

———. "William James, Positive Psychology, and Healthy-Mindedness." *The Journal of Speculative Philosophy (New Series),* 17 (2003): 53–67.

———. "William James's Divided Self and the Process of Its Unification: A Reply to Richard Gale." *Transactions of the Charles S. Peirce Society,* 39 (2003): 645–56.

———. "Is Healthy-Mindedness Healthy?" *Cross Currents,* 53 (2003): 404–12.

———. "William James and the Journey toward Unification." *Transactions of the Charles S. Peirce Society,* 40 (2004): 787–802. Perry, Ralph Barton. *The Thought and Character of William James.* 2 vols. Boston: Little, Brown, 1935.

Plato. *Parmenides.* In *The Dialogues of Plato.* Vol. 2. Translated by B. Jowett. New York: Random House, 1892.

———. *Symposium.* In *The Dialogues of Plato.* Vol. 1. Translated by B. Jowett. New York: Random House, 1892. 301–45.

Popper, Karl, Sir. "Philosophy of Science: A Personal Report." In *British Philosophy in the Mid-Century,* edited by C. A. Mace, 155–91. London: Allen and Unwin, 1957.

Potter, Vincent G., and Paul B. Shields, "Peirce's Definitions of Continuity." *Transactions of the Charles S. Peirce Society* 13 (1977): 20–34.

Ruf, Frederick J. *The Creation of Chaos: William James and the Stylistic Making of a Disorderly World.* Albany: State University of New York Press, 1991.

Russell, Bertrand. *A History of Western Philosophy.* New York: Simon and Schuster, 1945.

Seigfried, Charlene Haddock. *William James's Radical Reconstruction of Philosophy.* Albany: State University of New York Press, 1990.

Shakespeare, William. *Romeo and Juliet.* In *The Riverside Shakespeare*, edited by G. Blakemore Evans, 1058–99. Boston: Houghton Mifflin, 1974.

———. *The Two Gentlemen of Verona.* In *The Riverside Shakespeare*, edited by G. Blakemore Evans, 147–73. Boston: Houghton Mifflin, 1974.

Smith, John E. *The Spirit of American Philosophy.* Albany: State University of New York Press, 1983.

Suckiel, Ellen Kappy. *The Pragmatic Philosophy of William James.* Notre Dame, IN: University of Notre Dame Press, 1982.

———. *Heaven's Champion: William James's Philosophy of Religion.* Notre Dame, IN: University of Notre Dame Press, 1996.

Thayer, H. S. *Meaning and Action: A Critical History of Pragmatism.* 2nd ed. Indianapolis: Hackett, 1981.

Wordsworth, William. "Composed Upon Westminster Bridge, Sept. 3, 1802." *The Complete Poetical Works of William Wordsworth.* New York: Thomas Y. Crowell, n.d. 207.

Index

absolute idealism. *See* idealism, absolute

absolutism, mystical. *See* mysticism: "anti-Promethean"

action: ideomotor, 50, 54, 134, 145; deliberative, 50; moral (*see* morality)

agnostic positivism, 13

alternative healing, 19

Allen, Grant, 7

Anti-Imperialist League, 19

anti-intellectualism. *See* intellectualism

Aquinas. *See* Thomas Aquinas, Saint

Aristotle, 98, 148–49

attention, 34, 52–53, 112, 123, 167n13, 168n6: effort of, 55–56; and genius, 67, 145–46

Augustine, Saint, 143, 155–56

Berkeley, George, 74

Bible, The, 136, 148–49, 151, 152

Bixler, Julius, 68–69, 101, 104–5, 109, 166–67nn12–14, 168n4, 170n1

Bradley, F. H., 84

Breakfast Club, The, 140

Buddha, 20, 71, 78

Bunyan, John, 78

"cash value," xvi, xix, 129

Calvin, John, 26

Cantor, Georg, 165n2

Capps, John, 170n21

Christianity, 74, 78. *See also* Bible, The; Jesus

church, xvi, 4, 18, 64: as guardian of social evolution, 27; as inessential to religion, 21

Clifford, William Kingdon, 12–13, 41

conception, xvii, 31: attenuated role of in *Varieties of Religious Experience*, 60–61, 63–65; as department of self, 37, 39–44; and epiphanic experience, 143; excised from reflex arc, 109; fallibility of, 165n1; integration with perception, 115, 120; and religion, 70; as secondary to perception, 120; as secondary to volition, 119; as selection, 34. *See also* perception; reflex action model; volition

consciousness: active element of, 123; impulsiveness of, 50; and panpsychism, 87–88; as part of continuum, 90; personal, 36; stream of (*see* stream of consciousness); unnamed states of, 33

conversion: in epiphany, 14; religious, 67, 71–74, 79–82, 90

Cooper, Wesley, 100–1, 170n10

cycle of operation, 5–7, 125: of genius, 9, 160; in James's psychology, 54–55

cynicism: as response to epiphany, 142, 157

Danisi, John, xiii

Darwin, Charles, 5–6, 8, 10

decision-making: 50–52

179